A Guide to Socially-Informed Research for Architects and Designers

This book offers an efficient set of step-by-step tips and overarching lessons about how to gather useful, meaningful, and socially-informed data about clients' and other stakeholders' experiences in architecture and interior design professions.

In this guide, author Michelle Janning helps the design professional conduct ongoing evaluation of design projects, create useful pre- and post-design evaluations, frame effective questions for improved future design, involve various stakeholders in the research process, and focus on responsible and evidence-based human-centered design to improve the relationship between design and people's experiences. Examining a variety of both large- and small-scale project examples from different institutional realms, including healthcare sites, schools, residences, eating establishments, museums, and theaters, this book highlights not only the overlap in these types of projects but also the differences between project sizes that may impact the methods used in any given project. It also offers tools for how to communicate design success to audiences that include potential clients, occupants, and other designers.

A Guide to Socially-Informed Research for Architects and Designers is a go-to reference for design professionals interested in using accessible social scientific methods to gather essential and practical information from people who occupy the spaces they design and to do so in an ethical, inclusive, and socially-informed way in order to enhance social sustainability in the built environment.

Michelle Janning is the Raymond and Elsie DeBurgh Chair of Social Sciences and Professor of Sociology at Whitman College.

A Guide to Socially-Informed Research for Architects and Designers

MICHELLE JANNING

NEW YORK AND LONDON

Designed cover image: Allison Wanichek

First published 2023
by Routledge
605 Third Avenue, New York, NY 10158

and by Routledge
4 Park Square, Milton Park, Abingdon, Oxon, OX14 4RN

Routledge is an imprint of the Taylor & Francis Group, an informa business

© 2023 Michelle Janning

The right of Michelle Janning to be identified as author of this work has been asserted in accordance with sections 77 and 78 of the Copyright, Designs and Patents Act 1988.

All rights reserved. No part of this book may be reprinted or reproduced or utilised in any form or by any electronic, mechanical, or other means, now known or hereafter invented, including photocopying and recording, or in any information storage or retrieval system, without permission in writing from the publishers.

Trademark notice: Product or corporate names may be trademarks or registered trademarks, and are used only for identification and explanation without intent to infringe.

Library of Congress Cataloging-in-Publication Data
Names: Janning, Michelle Yvonne, author.
Title: A guide to socially-informed research for architects and designers / Michelle Janning.
Description: New York: Routledge, 2023. | Includes index. | Identifiers: LCCN 2022026111 | ISBN 9781032023977 (hardback) | ISBN 9781032023984 (paperback) | ISBN 9781003183228 (ebook)
Subjects: LCSH: Architecture–Research–Methodology. | Architectural practice–Social aspects.
Classification: LCC NA1995 .J36 2023 | DDC 720.72–dc23/eng/20220720
LC record available at https://lccn.loc.gov/2022026111

ISBN: 978-1-032-02397-7 (hbk)
ISBN: 978-1-032-02398-4 (pbk)
ISBN: 978-1-003-18322-8 (ebk)

DOI: 10.4324/9781003183228

Typeset in Avenir and Dante
by codeMantra

This book is dedicated to everyone who loves the design of data and the data of design.

Contents

List of Tables		*viii*
Acknowledgments		*ix*
	Introduction: Incorporating Socially-Informed Research into Design – The WHY	**1**
1	Framing a Project's Goals and Research Question – The WHAT	30
2	Choosing a Research Method to Inform Design – The HOW	52
3	Choosing a Sample and Communicating with People during the Research Process – The WHO	76
4	Setting and Pace for Data Collection – The WHERE and WHEN	97
5	Telling the Data Story with Analysis and Presentation – Continuing the HOW	118
	Conclusion: Informing Future Design and Designing Socially Sustainable Communities – Revisiting the WHY	**141**
	Glossary	*157*
	Index	*165*

Tables

1 Projects Informing This Book 14
2 Benefits and Drawbacks of Methods 55

Acknowledgments

I am grateful for the support, suggestions, and rapid response to questions from the past and present editorial team in the Routledge architecture titles section, which includes Krystal Racaniello, Christine Bondira, and Jake Millicheap. I'm also thankful to the anonymous reviewers who helped me move the project from proposal to manuscript in ways that made sense to professionals in varied design fields. And many thanks go to Allison Wanichek, who designed the wonderful cover for this book, where my only instruction was "please design something that says 'data meets design.'"

My Whitman College colleagues and students who constantly inspire and teach me about sociological research methods, social inequalities, human-centered design, and ethics have been instrumental in helping me think through a lot of the ideas in this book. I am grateful to Alzada Tipton, who serves as Whitman's Provost and Dean of the Faculty, and who has provided funding for my efforts related to this book. And I am indebted to Peter Harvey, Nancy Tavelli, and Dalia Corkrum for inviting me to participate as a community member and consultant on many design projects at Whitman College over the past two decades.

Many people agreed to be interviewed or have their ideas shared in this book, for which I am immensely grateful. These include individuals from diverse professions who have captivating stories about design, building, health, social justice, community development, qualitative research, museum curatorial and management work, market research, and interior design and architecture professional standards and shifts. Thank you to Lynne Jensen-Nelson, Lori Bettison-Varga, Romano Nickerson, Marty Janning, Neal Christopherson, Shelby Blessing, Jaimie Thimmesh Rachie, and McKenna

Vetter. I have also been inspired by architect Braulio Baptista and designers Molly Kidd and Robin Daly by talking with them informally and viewing their varied projects wherein they create beautiful and inclusive spaces for people from many walks of life.

I'm so fortunate to have great friends and a loving and supportive family, including my mom and brothers (and their families) and my husband's family, all of whom know how much I love design and architecture and have always supported my thirst to combine this love with the sociological part of my brain. Thanks go to my son Aaron and my son-for-a-year Mohamed Ali, both of whom have had to put up with me writing much of this book in the dining room, which is a space arguably more suited to afterschool and late-night snacking than to writing. Special shout out to Aaron, by the way, who also astutely noted that pointing out the multiple uses of our dining room in this Acknowledgments section actually aligns with the goals of this book. Finally, I am so thankful to my husband Neal, who has served as a built-in sociological research methods expert and extra-generous partner in household tasks for the last two years so I could focus on teaching, research, and writing made more challenging by a global pandemic.

Introduction
Incorporating Socially-Informed Research into Design – The WHY

Why Was I Inspired to Write This Book?

In 2017, I meandered through an exhibit entitled "A Real Danish Family" in the National Gallery of Art in Copenhagen, Denmark (in Danish: Statens Museum for Kunst, or SMK). In this exhibit, a collection of artists and social scientists collaborated on a visual representation of the changing diversity of family types and definitions in Denmark. On the white gallery walls were representative quotes from interviews, colorful charts, infographics visualizing population changes in Denmark, interactive exhibits for children to pose questions and offer their definitions of family, photographs of families, and a photo of artist Gillian Wearing's sculpture of the family chosen to represent "A Real Danish Family" (which was situated outside the museum), and other art pieces by Wearing organized in a neighboring gallery as "Family Stories." Alongside artists' names were the names of university anthropologists and sociologists who offered their rendition of current family stories through updated data. It was in this exhibit where I realized that social science data could be presented using beautiful and aesthetically compelling design, and that art could be crafted and organized systematically – both to tell a complex and curated story of changing social patterns. It was in this exhibit where I witnessed – more vividly than I had in the past – design meeting data.

I've lived, taught, and conducted research off and on in Denmark over the last decade, paying close attention to Danish design in toys and furniture and to interdisciplinary research on social behaviors in the Scandinavian context. I have observed how LEGO designers monitor changing constructions of

DOI: 10.4324/9781003183228-1

childhood in the creation of new bricks, how minimalist design pairs with social patterns in cold and dark times of the year, how old buildings with crooked floors and low ceilings are like comfortable blankets when candlelit on a dark winter evening, and how urban parks with plenty of bicycle parking foster interaction rather than isolation in various Copenhagen neighborhoods. But it was the exhibit at the SMK that deepened the fusion of art, design, and *sociology* – the systematic study of human group behavior – for me. I aim for this book to do the same for readers.

A few months after my interlude with Gillian Wearing's sculpture and the infographics telling the story of "A Real Danish Family," I was sitting in the pristine board room of a downtown architecture firm in an Austin, Texas high rise. I had been given a tour of a couple of firms by Shelby Blessing (a former student of mine) as a way to introduce me to the spaces in which architects work and to give me a glimpse of her work world. But the project we were discussing in that board room was not firm-specific, nor was the meeting held in the midst of a flurry of architecture and design professionals busy at work on a weekday. Instead, I was seated at boardroom table on a sunny Sunday afternoon with architects representing two different firms, non-profit volunteers, and architecture students, all of whom were part of a community project devoted to studying how well a new microhome community for disabled and chronically homeless individuals had been working for its residents. This group, nearly ready to collect some good *post-occupancy data* (data collected after people have moved into a building or design once completed), had asked me to talk with them about ways to interview residents to make sure they asked the right questions, treated the residents equitably, talked to enough people, and got good data so that the next design phase would be even better. As the two-hour session transpired, it became apparent that they had marvelous ideas for gathering data, but also that some relatively manageable methodological adjustments would make the project even better. I was excited to participate in these conversations where we ended up synthesizing ideas into a more cohesive methodological approach that would yield good data, respect the residents, and capture the project's central goals in a systematic and productive way. The project continued with refined interview questions, enhanced ethical approaches to interviewing meant to empathize with residents, and some creative options that they hadn't thought of and that they could pair with mapping and a survey. As a result of the good work of this team, the new designs and community improvements became informed by a rigorous, meaningful, and manageable set of data that has been useful for many of their other projects. They already had a decent grasp of how well the design was working for residents in the community because their starting point for the research was well-articulated and thoughtful, and they were dedicated to ensuring the residents' experiences were positive. But it was apparent that a thoughtful and directed conversation about research methods could make things even better. Why not make a few simple changes to make the data not only more sophisticated but also more grounded in an empathetic understanding of end users? To do so improves every design project and informs subsequent designs.

It was in this session that it occurred to me that architects and designers collect data all the time (even if they don't always call it that), and spend countless hours deliberating about the relationship between their creations and our social worlds. I had seen this in my consultancy work, where the normal way of making design decisions was to ask people questions about how they view the design at each stage, and then pair that information with design expertise and attention to sustainability and safety and legal requirements. I had seen this in the numerous research studies produced by design professionals and scholars that I've been citing in my own academic work for years. But I have observed that the methods used and the ways in which the methods take place in these kinds of projects could use more conversations with social scientists. I could see that the form and function of a design necessarily need to be assessed by the designers themselves, but when it came to how people used and viewed the design, rigorous and thoughtful social science methods would come in handy.

Fast forward to 2021 and 2022, when I co-led a faculty and staff project at my own institution to develop an academic program in *human-centered design* (HCD) within a liberal arts context. The project was dedicated to creating an academic curriculum that helps students learn how to think about the creation of any artifact (e.g., a building or room, a website, or even a new system of client intake for a local non-profit organization) in terms of design and user experience. Part of the curriculum was about design and methods for data collection related to the user experience. I came to learn that this field of study offers a lovely way to blend design and social science – study what users want, need, and do in order to inform design, then maintain an iterative collection of user experiences at multiple stages in the design process (including after a design is completed) in order to inform future design. And while you're at it, use good design principles for the project itself – how to visually represent data, how to organize files, and so on. While HCD (sometimes in the form of UX [user experience design]) is present in the world of for-profit corporations and the tech industry, I realized that the principles guiding the intersection of design and assessment of the human experience of that design could be applied to many fields, and to objects that are physical rather than digital. In fact, HCD has always been informed by the architecture and design fields (Dam and Siang 2022), so this revelation was not exactly new. But I also realized that architects and designers may be helped by knowing more about ways to gather data on user experience at the same time sociologists may be helped by informing the design process itself in order to create positive social change in our world. In essence, I saw a need for a one-stop shop for how design and social science may intersect, which is the aim of this book.

These experiences called to mind some conversations about architecture and interior design I have had over the years with designers, academic researchers, and friends. Those conversations usually include claims like these:

- "I'm a creative person; I don't do data."
- "Our data-driven culture is lessening spontaneity and redefining the creative process as something that is to be counted and organized. There is no such thing as evidence-based design."
- "Design should not come with customer satisfaction surveys."
- "How we use designed spaces is more about stories than statistics."

Or sometimes the claim sounds like this:

- "Data has to be quantitative and analyzed using statistical significance procedures in order for me to use it to inform design."

The first few of these quotes are about the creeping in of market forces and data-driven practices that seem to run counter to thinking about design as an art, or as entirely subjective. But the last one indicates the view that evidence used to inform the design process has to be formal and rigid, as if the data will be used in a peer-reviewed scientific academic article. I think a balance between all of these is needed. We live in a world filled with satisfaction surveys, misuse and misunderstanding (and politically charged use) of data, and fear that arts and creative fields in our schools are being lost at the expense of "hard sciences." At the same time, we in higher education see a call for more rigorous efforts to enhance numeric and information literacy among students. To me, any effort that we can make to capture stories and data, with a lot of rigor, compassion, empathy, and an eye toward being systematic and interdisciplinary, would address these issues. We need data, and we need stories. There is no reason not to have both, and it is in the design world where these two can be integrated in fulfilling ways.

Regardless of which quotes, if any, may resonate with you, suffice it to say that design and data may not be as mutually exclusive as our world sometimes presents, and data doesn't have to be made up entirely of numbers and statistics. The interplay between design and data-driven and socially-informed research is complex. Below I define socially-informed research and outline my assumptions and motivations guiding this book as a way for you to see how I approach this complexity.

Why Should Architects and Designers Conduct Socially-Informed Research (and What Is It)?

Socially-informed research in design is the ethical and intentional incorporation of human-centered data gathering and analysis throughout the design process. It is the iterative and systematic practice of gathering, analyzing, and sharing input from people who occupy and engage with the built environments that architects and interior designers create as the designs are created and built. The research process focuses not just on personal preferences and psychological impacts but also on an understanding of group inequalities, social systems, and cultural contexts that shape preferences. Conducting socially-informed research in the design process enhances the sustainability of our rooms, buildings, neighborhoods, and communities, because current and future projects are informed not just by the expertise of the designers and individual psychological factors of people who engage with a design, but also by the values and social locations of people who will inhabit and use the design over time and the social and cultural context in which the design resides. Socially-informed design is similar to participatory design (Mahabadi et al. 2014), which invites community engagement and responsibility in the design process, but I frame and elaborate it here with a specific dedication to using ethical and rigorous sociological methods to do so, and with a focus on multiple methods and design contexts.

Socially-informed design is growing in popularity and application, and current events in the fields of architecture and design speak to this emphasis. For example, the 2022 Pritzker Prize in architecture was awarded to Francis Kéré, the first African to win the esteemed prize. The prize has traditionally honored architects whose buildings were flashy and iconic, which differs from Kéré's decidedly socially-oriented designs relating to education, health care, and community development in his home community of Gando in Burkina Faso. Two decades ago when he designed and built a school in the community where he was raised – a community that did not have a school when he lived there as a child – his career was launched (Holland 2022). The recent recognition of his work suggests that values of community, access, and social equality (not to mention a global focus) are now permeating the field. Because of this increasing focus on socially-informed design, I aim to offer a book that guides designers through research techniques that are themselves socially-informed.

As sociologists have been noting for nearly two decades, the links between our field and design professions are obvious. I see it as a calling for us to help others "see the relationship between social setting and the individual and organization," thereby contributing to important work outside of the field of sociology (Beaman 2002). Sociology is a useful lens to apply to socially-informed design, as designer (and trained sociologist) Fauzia Khanani articulated in a recent issue of *Interior Design*:

> We incorporate social science research methods before, during and after the design process—things like looking at case studies and related research, interviewing clients and conducting focus groups, and doing post-occupancy evaluations. From a public health perspective, I've always felt strongly that design affects the quality of life for those experiencing it. Research is finally emerging in support of the idea that the physical qualities of a space directly affect those that use it. Everything from the colors of walls to the textures of flooring, all of things we spend time designing, affect people so it's important that we create dynamic spaces that will promote change, heal or inspire.
>
> (Dorris 2016)

Thus, sociology and design professions already inform each other. My goal with this book is to add emphasis on the social research methods we employ that may help inform the design process.

Defining Research

Since the aim of this book is to talk about sociological research methods that can be used in the design process, I should unpack the word "research" a bit. According to etymonline.com, the term research (or recerche, in Old French) was used as early as the 1500s to mean "the act of searching closely" (as a noun) or "investigate or study (a matter) closely, search or examine with continued care" (as a verb). When students are assigned a "research" paper for their high school civics class, for example, it means they are required to investigate a topic using reputable sources, and then write a paper that summarizes or synthesizes what those sources say. In the paper, they would likely prioritize or highlight certain topics or claims above others, especially if the research is meant to point to some kind of persuasive argument. This kind of research requires effort, rigor, and depth, but it is usually limited to gathering and interpreting the past work of others in order to make certain claims.

We can also think of research in our everyday lives as gathering information that we'd use to make important decisions. So, for example, if we are buying a new car, we'd do our "research." We'd look at online reviews, seek input from friends about their experiences, compare prices, or go for some test drives. This kind of research may require effort, rigor, and depth, but it does not require being systematic and it is not something that is assigned to us by someone who will evaluate how well we've done our research. In this sense, "research" is more akin to its Latin root "circare" – to "go about, wander, traverse" (also where the word circus comes from) (etymonline.com).

For me, *research* has meant something a bit more specific, at least in terms of my professional work and the way I use it in this book (though I've done the kind of research noted in the previous paragraphs). Research involves (1) systematic (scientific, really) posing of a question that can be answered using quantitative or qualitative data, (2) gathering and analyzing that data, (3) presenting key findings as a way to answer the research question, and (4) interpreting those findings using concepts and theories that come from fields that relate to the question. So, for example, when I wanted to learn more about how COVID-19 impacted college students' experiences with learning in various living environments (at home, in a dormitory, in an apartment, etc.), I started by asking a few of my students how things were going. But that wasn't research yet (some may call it "anecdotal research" but I saw it more as conversation and a path to figuring out how I should frame my eventual research question). When I examined past published research and theories in fields that related to the topic and gathered a team of student research assistants, we were able to come up with a final research question, data-gathering and analysis plan, and likely audience for the study's findings (Janning et al. 2022).

How have architects and interior designers defined research, and is it the same as I'm using in this book? As architecture professor Ray Lucas (2016) notes in his book *Research Methods for Architecture*, the definition is multifaceted. On one hand, architecture is an academic discipline. *Architectural research* is studying the history of the field, understanding the social and cultural context and the role of buildings in these contexts, and testing and improving theories about "what it means to build and dwell" (7). Architecture is treated here as a "knowledge tradition" or "body of knowledge," just like chemistry or sociology, even though it is also a practice. Related to this, Lucas offers this formal definition of research:

> The process by which you understand the world in a verifiable and consistent manner…typically conducted by the application of an existing model to a new set of circumstances, or by developing a new framework from empirical facts. Merely collating information is not enough to constitute research, however – the aim is to say something meaningful as a result of the data gathered.
>
> (8)

This definition is similar to mine, especially in terms of the value of being systematic and embedding the question, data gathering, and analysis in a larger conceptual framework. But how useful is this definition of research for architects or designers who are not publishing peer-reviewed research or aiming to concertedly and publicly situate their work in a vast architectural knowledge tradition? How does research work for everyday architectural *practice*?

In order to unpack what counts as "meaningful" in research done solely in the realm of architecture and design practice, Lucas adds to his aforementioned definition that research can be conducted just by doing architectural design. He notes important overlaps between the often artificially-boundaried research and practice, saying that architects are constantly changing and critiquing designs as part of a "loop of reflective practice" (43). He elaborates:

> It is not enough for the production of architecture, be that through drawings, models, technologies or buildings, to be merely functional and in fulfillment of the brief. It must have value added in terms of an investigation that contributes to our knowledge of the discipline and the world at large.
>
> (43)

Sometimes this takes the form of an installation where viewers can reflect on the design, or even an interactive intervention or "happening" meant to provoke a response. Sometimes it occurs by virtue of the fact that designed buildings become part of the "library" of designs that future designers can use to inform their work. Ultimately Lucas argues that architectural practice already has elements of research and that it is important to apply findings from practical investigations in future designs. However, his book is still written as a guide for architects who want to be quite formal with their research with the goal of publishing and sharing knowledge within the discipline. And he frames social scientific research (usually sociological or anthropological) as useful for practitioners but mostly in the form of collaboration with sociologists and anthropologists. My take is a bit different insofar as I'd like architects and designers themselves to have the needed social scientific skills to do research that may inform current and future design and to possess these the moment they step into a practice or a project. The research process may or may not result in academic publishing.

There is ample existing research in architecture and interior design that has served these fields well, and that has informed design such that we see more nods to eradicating social inequalities and enhancing social and environmental sustainability. Sometimes this is done quite formally, with the goal of publishing the outcomes of an academic project to enhance the shared knowledge in the field. At other times it is more of a "noticing of patterns" that are part of a design or architecture practice: concertedly keeping track of people's views of the design as it gets revised based on input, and then making note of design that meets some kind of social need.

Importantly, the interior design profession has formalized the intersections between data and design. This is evidenced in the Council for Interior Design Accreditation 2020 Professional Standards. More specifically, Section II: *Knowledge Acquisition and Application* includes three standards that directly map onto the goals of this book. These include:

- Standard 7 "Human-Centered Design" includes a focus on the role of evidence in HCD ("Student work demonstrates the ability to: gather and apply human-centered evidence; analyse and synthesize human perception and behaviour patterns to inform design solutions") (II-20).
- Standard 8 "Design Process" includes the student learning outcomes that "Student work demonstrates the ability to apply knowledge and skills learned to: …synthesize information to generate evidence-based design solutions," and that "Students understand the importance of evaluating the relevance and reliability of information and research impacting design solutions" (II-21).
- Standard 9 "Communication" includes the student learning expectation that "Students are able to effectively interpret and communicate data and research" (II-23).

In addition to professional standards in design professions, there are ample resources on how research matters for architects and designers, including formal academic approaches and approaches that are directly mapped onto student learning goals in design classrooms. Best practices in research conducted in architecture and interior design can be found in the following sources if you'd like to explore further:

- The Quality of Life Foundation (https://www.qolf.org/)
- The UK Collaborative Centre for Housing Evidence (https://housingevidence.ac.uk/)
- The winning submission on "mapping social values" for the Cities and Communities theme of the 2020 Royal Institute of British Architects President's Awards for Research instructional article by Eli Hatleskog and Flora Samuel (2021)
- Fionn Stevenson's (2019) *Housing Fit for Purpose: Performance, Feedback and Learning*
- *The Social Value Toolkit for Architecture* created at the University of Reading with RIBA, which "has been developed to make it simple to evaluate and demonstrate the social impact of design on people and communities" (https://www.architecture.com/knowledge-and-resources/resources-landing-page/social-value-toolkit-for-architecture#:~:text=The%20Social%20Value%20Toolkit%20for, scores%20of%20bids%20and%20tenders)
- The American Institute of Architects research across three scales: occupant, building, and societal/community, which connects individual human behavior and needs (and neuroscience) with building and material performance and culture/community engagement to "improve equity and quality of life for all" (https://www.aia.org/pages/5626-architectural-research)
- Contract Design Network's "Designing Workplaces with Data" which elaborates ways to measure the success of workplace design using quantifiable data (https://www.contractdesign.com/practice/design/designing-workplaces-data/).
- Open Architecture Collaborative's video "Defining Your Focus: Assessment Tools" to figure out local needs during the design process using tools such as community mapping (https://www.youtube.com/watch?v=QW07IgnC6Jw&list=PLFi159qXw_vWCRimDkbLm5HACBNa1Ser0&index=1)
- Pathways to Equity program on best practices for community engagement and equitable design (https://www.pathwaystoequity.org/)

My aim is to blur not only the boundary between design research and practice (as Lucas does to some extent), but to also blur the boundary between architecture, design, and sociology (as the Council for Interior Design Accreditation

(CIDA) standards do). I also aim to infuse HCD (and UX) approaches into this book. Why can't architects and designers themselves learn how to conduct sociological research in their practice? Why can't designers learn how to think about and manage data from the people who will inhabit their designs? Why can't sociology and HCD intersect in ways that help create a better design? This book is informed by existing best practices in architecture and interior design research, but I bolster this by showing how sociological concepts and methods can improve upon existing good work. And I note ways that intersections between sociology and HCD can take designers one step further toward designing and building more sustainable and socially responsible spaces and places.

Before I delve into the guiding principles of this book, I want to offer a brief note about third-party players in the design/research partnership. I had a chance to talk with Dr. Lori Bettison-Varga, President and Director of the Natural History Museum (NHM) of Los Angeles County. Lori told me about a multi-year design project at the NHM that involved data gathering that informed the design development process of the exterior, building, and interior design of exhibitions and spaces for a project called NHM Commons. This data collection was not managed by the architectural firm working on the project, but rather by an outside firm. The NHM built on that data collection with additional methods to collect perspectives on a redesign of their second site, La Brea Tar Pits and Museum. Combined, they had collected a lot of data to then drive the selection process for the architectural competition for the Tar Pits project. In large multi-stage projects like this one, it is not unusual to hire an independent consulting firm as part of an assessment of community attitudes and experiences (along with views about light and noise and environmental sustainability) using some of the data-gathering methods I discuss in this book. Because the project that Lori described will be a large indoor/outdoor civic space meant to serve both museum visitors and local residents, community buy-in for the project was essential. And community buy-in required the NHM to ensure objectivity and a vision that put community needs above any desires of a particular architecture firm. In this case, the museum collected data telling the important story about local residents' relationship with nature and their desires for a community space. The community needs drove the design, and they continue to drive the long-term project as architecture and design professionals partner with the museum on the project. And so, for a large long-term project that is meant to meet the needs of broad and varied constituencies, sometimes the research part is done by people outside of the architecture and design fields. But at the same time, the architects and designers involved (and the museum partners) need to understand what data has been collected, what data is useful, and what ideas in the design process can inform further data collection.

For smaller firms and smaller projects, my hope is that this book provides enough instruction to be able to manage the socially-informed research process in-house, and in partnership with clients. But for larger projects where an independent entity may be doing the research, this book can provide a helpful framing and vocabulary so that any architect or designer working with data from people who will eventually engage with their design will know what the data says, and they'll know how to tell if the data is socially-informed.

Why Is This Book Important? Guiding Principles, Motivations, and Goals

I have three guiding principles underlying my approach to socially-informed research in the design process that are inspired by my experiences in Copenhagen and Austin, by my own work as a researcher and consultant, and by the many projects I've worked on and the many conversations I've had over the years with sociologists, architects, and designers:

1. Data can be dangerous when used without context, used incorrectly, or used for the wrong reason. So can design. Thus, it is important to think about ethics, the position of the designer, and the larger socio-political context in which the design is situated.
2. Design already has systematic elements that require organization, planning, and keeping track. And social science can include creativity, stories, and non-standardized approaches to gathering input from people. Designers can hone their data skills, and data people can hone their design skills, but this isn't always easy to see or do. Design and social science are not only compatible, they are two sides of the same coin. Wanting to improve social and physical conditions is a goal in both, but these two approaches may differ in how they try to achieve this. The coexistence of design and social science (especially sociology) as two prongs in a larger project toward sustainability, inclusivity, and socially-informed decisions for our rooms, buildings, neighborhoods, and communities requires honest and thoughtful translation across approaches. For this reason, it is important to see these professions as overlapping and integrated, despite disparate training, credentials, and audiences.
3. Figuring out whether something works beyond our own subjective assessment can help with revision and redesign when we try to do it again. This is not only useful to create designs that people use and enjoy; it is also an ethical responsibility to be empathetic to those people so that their values and desires can make the design useful and enjoyable. For

this reason, it is important to learn about social science methods alongside consideration of the research process as a social process itself.

This book synthesizes ideas I've collected over years of consultancies and dozens of my own research projects, and after a few inspiring moments where design and data merged in beautiful ways. I aim to bridge the worlds of social science (with a particular focus on sociology) and design. Good research about people's experiences helps designers and architects create useful, enjoyable, and sustainable designs, and sociologists are particularly good at studying people's roles, relationships, and the connections to larger groups that make up these experiences. But sociologists don't always know how design actually works or how our built environment is intimately connected to our social world, or that good research is already happening outside of our fields of expertise. I aim to bridge all of these worlds.

My approach to socially-informed research in design is motivated by four elements that lead to specific goals, listed here and elaborated below:

1. I am motivated by my gratitude and excitement at having worked on design projects with diverse people and within diverse settings, which leads to Goal #1: take into consideration the ways that social group inequality, history, and social systems shape people's values and access to desirable spaces and things.
2. I am motivated by my training as a sociologist, which leads to Goal #2: infuse a bit more sociology into the design process, both conceptually and methodologically.
3. I am motivated by my understanding of HCD, which leads to Goal #3: integrate successful HCD approaches with sociological research in the design process, thus approaching design using an integrative and interdisciplinary lens.
4. I am motivated by my belief that design should be iterative and formative, which leads to Goal #4: inform future design with research conducted as part of past and present design processes.

I have done a lot of professional work with designers and architects. In Table 1, I list several design projects I've worked on, usually with a team of designers, architects, and stakeholders, but sometimes just on my own or with other sociologists. With each item, I describe project goals and what research, practice, and pedagogical outlets were part of the project (e.g., just to inform the design itself, and/or to share widely as an academic paper). To be clear, I served as a lead on the sociological research projects noted but did not serve as a lead designer or manager of any of the designs. The following list shows the types of projects that have informed many of the examples I use in this book to illustrate concepts and methods.

Below I elaborate on the four motivations and goals described earlier, highlighting the past projects featured in Table 1.

Table 1 Projects Informing This Book

Type of Building/Space	Socially-Informed Project Goals	Research, Practice, and Pedagogical Outcomes
College Residence Halls	Creating community, safety, and a sense of home within college student residence halls and off-campus housing	New residence hall built; published academic article
Shared Dining Facilities	Establishing social connections within communal dining establishments and cohousing communities	New dining hall built; published book chapter
Preschools	Comparing childhood independence in preschools cross-nationally (US and Denmark)	Creation of an academic course in sociology and design in childhood
Private Home Spaces	Finding work/school-family balance for family members who share learning/paid work spaces (including during the COVID-19 pandemic); creating positive family roles and relationships within domestic interiors	Creation of work/life balance in home spaces workshop; published academic articles, chapters, and book
Home Spaces and Museums/Galleries	Understanding the curation and display of digital and paper mementos for collective and private memory (private and in museum curatorial work)	Published multiple academic articles and book; co-curated a museum exhibit on war and memory
Microhome Communities	Establishing independence and connectedness for disabled and chronically homeless individuals within a microhome community	Community designed and constructed
Health Care Settings	Infusing art and design in health care settings to enhance patient mental health	Workplace workshop created
Private Homes	Downsizing and sorting through family possessions including heirloom art pieces to prevent clutter	Academic articles published and lectures given
School Classrooms and Libraries	Creating optimal learning environments in classrooms and libraries	Redesigned use of space in classroom building and library
Vacation Homes and Neighborhoods	Understanding tourism, neighborhood cohesiveness, and décor in vacation and short-term rental homes	Blog posts written, book project

1. Take into consideration the ways that social group inequality, history, and social systems shape people's values and access to desirable spaces and things.

As I have worked on the projects listed in Table 1, I have collected stories about how the design process is not just about aesthetics and functions for individual users; it is also about fostering inclusivity and sustainability on a collective level and working on ways to eradicate social inequalities that our built environment has created or fostered. This conclusion stems directly from my experience with design processes that have included input from every stakeholder group – even and especially ones made up of people who have less ability to speak up – as part of the process. My ideas also come from conference and workshop sessions I've attended, conversations I've had with design, building, and architecture professionals (or organizational leaders who've worked on design projects), and professional organizations that I'm part of (or that I reference in my own work). Importantly, a lot of the ideas I present here come from more than two decades of my own experience teaching research methods and working as a social science consultant on design projects. But a lot is inspired by others.

As The Constructed Environment's website notes:

> As human artifice, our various design and construction practices shape our lives. The physical forms they leave are a humanistic legacy. However, our human experiences and interests are irreducibly diverse. So how does a constructed environment affect different people differentially? How can it be sensitive to their varied needs? How can it be inclusive? How can potentially negative impacts be anticipated and mitigated? How can a constructed environment be designed and made in such a way as to best serve the panoply of human needs?
> (https://constructedenvironment.com/about/scope-concerns)

You cannot design a helpful learning space without considering people's experiences with learning differences and ways that school context may or may not stigmatize these. You cannot design a living room storage unit without examining the ways that household roles may be divided by age or gender, especially when compared to past generations. You cannot look at how vacation homes are decorated without understanding how social class may allow some people to afford the homes in a gentrified neighborhood or community in the first place. And you cannot design a college residence hall that is meant to foster community without considering ways that race has historically impacted students' sense of inclusion and exclusion. In other words, designing with the user in mind is more than just about that user's psychological or personal experience. It is also about the social structures and systems (and group inequalities) in place that impact that experience. And the research process itself needs to foster inclusivity so that design does not reinforce or exacerbate existing inequalities. This book, then, centers unequal access to resources as salient not just for the end design but for the collaborative process of formulating the design itself.

2. Infuse a bit more sociology into the design process, both conceptually and methodologically.

As much as past projects that I've been involved with have yielded good dialogue and design (and research), I am often left wishing the data-gathering techniques that were used to inform the design would have been more akin to what I was used to as a social scientist. I wanted it to be more intentional, more systematic, more transparent about how input would be used, more explicit in terms of how data gathering was part of the social process of building designer-client-user relationships and more rigorous in terms of question framing and data analysis. I also wanted to see how data gathering in one design project could inform decisions in another project. I was not interested in making all of this more challenging or more in-depth in terms of fancy statistics or methods that require lots of extra training; rather, I was interested in making the gathering of input during a design process more robust, systematic, and transparent. I wanted to beef up the ways that both quantitative and qualitative feedback could be used in tandem to inform design. And I wished that it was more apparent to participants how their feedback (the "data") may actually be ethically used in the designs. Because of this, I discuss best practices in sociological research methods as they may inform design.

3. Integrate successful human-centered design approaches with sociological research in the design process, thus approaching design using an integrative and interdisciplinary lens.

At the same time that I wished past design projects would include more robust attention to rigorous sociological methods; I also wanted to learn from the interdisciplinary techniques used by practitioners in these settings, some of which align with methods used in HCD. In fact, HCD more generally emerged from architecture and design professions decades before we had heard of anything called an "app" or a "website" (Dam and Siang 2022). In these fields, a large sample size and robust statistical techniques are not necessarily required to make design decisions along the way. Nielsen (2000) has even suggested that in some cases input from five people is enough, though this is disputed and complicated, as outlined in Chapter 3. People's stories or the subjective retelling of their experience with a design are often as useful as a more scientific approach. Humans are not necessarily rational, consistent, or predictable in all cases, so social scientific methods can only go so far when it comes to capturing the subjective user experience with a space or building. Plus, sociology is not the only place HCD researchers look when deciding what methods to use; it is helpful to use a data-gathering method that best answers the question you're trying to answer. This method may include ideas from sociology (e.g., surveys), psychology (e.g., experiments), geography (e.g., mapping), anthropology (e.g., ethnography), communications (e.g., journals or word associations), or any combination of these and other fields. As a result of all of this, the next chapters detail ways that HCD (and UX) methods can complement sociological research methods used in the design process.

4. Inform future design with research conducted as part of past and present design processes.

In addition to being motivated by my own disciplinary training in sociology and ways to revise it using techniques already present in the design world, I also am dedicated to formative design: paying attention to past and present design to inform not just the next design phase but also the next set of design projects. I'm not the only one who thinks architecture and interior design professionals need to do a better job of using data from previous projects to inform future projects and to improve over time. Hay, Samuel, Watson, and Bradbury (2018) articulate that "[l]earning from previous projects systematically is central to improving building performance, resulting in a built environment that better fits the needs of clients, end users, wider society and the environment" (698). The authors claim that design professionals do not do enough systematic and consistent post-design evaluation in their practices and that the work that is being done on the complex intersections between design and people's experiences is housed primarily in academic research. Further, they suggest that improved systematic methods in these kinds of evaluations have resulted in improved design and better evidence for architecture and design professionals to use in the justification for investment in high-quality design. Indeed, even design professional organizations have created standards for accreditation to ensure tomorrow's designers and architects know what data is, how it works, how to use it, and how to communicate about it. This book offers an easy-to-follow way to fill the gap between these good ideas for evidence-based design in the everyday work of designers and architects and sound academic thinking on social scientific research methods, all as a way to inform future design to make it socially sustainable.

Why Does Sociology Help Us Understand Design?

Socially-informed research in architecture and interior design is about values and methods, and how these should inform each other. It occurs when designers and sociologists fulfill an ethical obligation not only to take into consideration the values and social locations of people who will engage with a design but also broader values about sustainability and eradication of social inequalities that can sometimes get missed when focusing too much on individual people. And these considerations are part of every step of a socially-informed research process, which the next chapters detail.

Earlier I defined socially-informed research for architects and designers as the ethical and intentional incorporation of sociological research methods in the design process. Sociology is the scientific study of human group behavior. We study people when they form groups of at least two or three (e.g., a family), and we study groups that include millions of people (e.g., a nation-state). We study social systems, and the pattern of relationships and networks between people as individuals, groups, organizations, and even large communities (e.g., a school system made up of teachers, students, administrators, families, and governmental branches that deal with property taxes and learning standards, as well as the relationship between all of these). I've heard my students call sociology the "psychology of groups." But this is oversimplified. We can include individual-level data in our research, and then we can cluster groups of individuals based on some characteristic that we think is important. When we group people together, we can see patterns in terms of whether one group differs from another. For example, we know from decades of research that, despite preferences that seem personal, patterns emerge about how people use their home spaces. My own research shows that women and men use home spaces differently, whether it's the greater likelihood for men to manage spaces where power tools reside or the greater likelihood for women to feel responsible for managing the aesthetics of home décor and family kinship keeping (Janning and Brambrink 2015; Janning and Menard 2006), even in a world where gender roles have been changing.

Our social world is ever-changing even as the buildings we live in seem fixed. Sociologists are adept at noticing how human behavior is (or is not) changing, but we don't as frequently notice the ways our built environment could revise or improve that behavior. Architects and designers are particularly adept at noticing how our built environment and objects align or misalign with human behavior, but don't as frequently know why human group behavior operates the way it does.

In the design examples that I intersperse throughout this book, I focus on the importance of the architect or designer knowing how to assess personal experiences that make someone enjoy or want to use a designed space or object. These experiences are already captured in lots of design research, and they likely are part of most designers' practice. But this kind of focus tends to be on the individual or psychological experience and impact only. For example, a certain photograph may elicit comfort or agitation in someone who enters a room where the photograph is displayed. Or a quilt may feel better to one person than another based on their personal preferences about color patterns, sleeping habits, or even body temperature. These are important elements of the design impact to capture since no design will work well if people don't feel good using or inhabiting that design. But they're not enough, because they don't take into account the larger social processes that may impact personal preferences in the first place.

Students of HCD learn about how important it is to capture the user experience during iterative phases of a design project (often these are designs for websites or apps, but the process holds true for any kind of design). The usability of any design depends on its features and on the user's desires and environment. This is something we have all probably realized, even unconsciously, when we get impatient with a website that is not loading because we don't have a lot of time or privacy, and we give up and move to the next site. But this individual lens is also limited.

While individual differences in experiences with design matter (and whereas people for whom designs are created want to feel as if their individual needs are met), designers also have a responsibility to pay attention to social and *cultural contexts* (shared value, belief, and language systems) and *social structures* (ways that society is organized), and *social inequalities* (when groups have unequal access to valuable resources such as money, space, or time). We need to situate individual preferences in a larger social context or the understanding of that experience is incomplete. Whereas psychology helps us understand attitudes, behaviors, and experiences from an individual perspective (at times in certain social contexts), sociology helps us understand the bigger picture.

Let's take the example of a displayed photograph eliciting certain emotions to illustrate the importance of social and cultural context. It may come as a surprise to learn that emotions are actually studied by sociologists. How so? How can something that feels so private actually tell a story about groups of people? In my research (Janning and Volk 2017) on college students' conceptions of home, a lot of survey respondents noted that the items they brought from home to college were meant to make a proud statement about their identity as either children or adults. For students who wanted to craft new adult identities, the photographs and other decorations they displayed tended to showcase their new interests (e.g., pictures at music concerts, travel pictures during a gap year). For students who were still emotionally connected to their families and were not concerned about showing their childhood selves to roommates or new college friends, the photographs they brought showed off their childhood experiences and preferences (e.g., a trip to Disneyland, a photo of a school club they participated in). When my students had to take their courses online from home during Fall 2020 (due to COVID-19), I recall talking with them about whether and how they chose to hide or display décor items that were in the background of the Zoom screen. For some students who did not have the opportunity to have a geographic move to college, and for whom crafting a new visible adult identity mattered, they hid their Disney princess posters and middle school sports trophies. So, emotions such as embarrassment and pride mattered to individual students in these scenarios.

An individual approach to preferences surrounding the display of childhood photos or objects during college would focus on the idiosyncratic differences from one student to the next. A sociological approach would embed those preferences into a larger social context where: (a) the transition from childhood to adulthood is socially significant, especially in contemporary US society; (b) a move to college is a visible marker of that transition; and (c) COVID-19 threw a wrench in the capacity of young people to pursue typically visible markers of the transition to adulthood, so they were collectively faced with new decisions about how to represent home spaces to new adult classmates. Whether a student was proud or embarrassed to show a childhood memento in a dorm room or on a Zoom screen has to be situated in the larger social context that shapes definitions of childhood and adulthood.

A sociological approach also focuses on social inequalities. Not everyone has equal access to good design, especially if there's a high price tag attached to it. Plus, defining design as "good" has historically been done by people in privileged positions. If a student brings a quilt from home, it may be because it's soft and warm and made special because it was crafted by a family member. Or the student may simply like the colors and patterns. These are personal reasons why the quilt made its way into a dormitory room. But a more complete picture of the quilt's journey from childhood home to dorm room would include: (a) pressure that a student may feel about adhering to norms surrounding what counts as "good dorm room décor;" (b) a student's access to financial resources that may allow purchasing a new set of bedding (in my writing I've called this "thread count capital" – it's expensive to have a high thread count; this is based on social theorist Pierre Bourdieu's (1985) concept of *cultural capital* – the social, material, and even linguistic resources someone has that makes others see them as having higher status, which in turn brings them even more resources); and (c) the availability of certain types of blankets and bedding in a specific time period, economic marketplace, and geographic context.

Clearly, objects tell a personal story, but they also tell a larger story. Spaces and buildings do this, too. A home office during COVID-19 may be constructed because of an individual family's needs, but the construction depends on their financial resources, spatial access, pressures from their workplaces about how much home and work time and spaces can intersect (and for how long), age and gender role expectations about who is more entitled to paid work spaces in a home, and historical and geographic context that may limit or grant access to technology needs, and that may heighten or limit expectations to create a home office based on social norms or market availability of supplies or builders. The meaning of a home space that is to be transformed for non-home purposes is influenced heavily by larger social forces, including the marketplace of available goods and workers to create or redesign a space, the social network of designers (Becker 1982) who are increasingly specialized and who shape tastes and preferences (Jones 1984), and the structure of the paid (digital and physical) work world that dictates where and how people are supposed to be working.

To consider these larger social forces while also understanding a personal story about objects or spaces requires using what sociologist C. Wright Mills (1959) calls the *sociological imagination*: a skill that allows us to understand any experience by considering both personal stories and the larger social and historical contexts in which those stories take place. Possessing the sociological imagination gives us the ability to notice the "little things of everyday life" and "subtle signals" of how and why a design may or may not work, even if the people engaging with the design may not even notice these signals (Sok 2018). This "noticing" is sometimes called *defamiliarization* (Bauman and May 2019), which allows us to understand the underlying structures of our social world by puzzling over taken-for-granted aspects. These subtle and even invisible things – cultural rules for how we live together, social roles prescribed by our group identities, and social location based on finances, gender, or other demographic traits – are what sociologists notice when they tell the story of how a design is or is not working. My aim with this book is to show how designers can also possess the sociological imagination and take a step back to notice structures and collective patterns that inform personal design preferences.

Why Learn from Human-Centered Design and Applied Sociology?

In 2021 and 2022 I had an opportunity to participate in a workshop at my institution with faculty members across a variety of academic disciplines – digital art, language and literature, theater set design, digital music production, computer science, museum studies, economics, psychology, and anthropology – in order to figure out if our college could create a new academic program for students. We focused on intersections of design, computer science, and social science data collection in our efforts to frame a program in human-centered design. But what exactly did we mean by this? Was this supposed to be a way to teach how market research fits into the design of computer applications? Or to teach business tactics to artists? Or to just call attention to the ubiquity of technology in our everyday lives? Short answer: not really any of these. Instead, our goal was to find a way to teach students design (how do you make a website, or app, or recording, or theater prop, or any digital or physical artifact, or any social system meant to meet some kind of need?) alongside critical thinking (who is best served by this design, who are the people involved in creating and how do inequalities and networks matter in this creation, what is our ethical responsibility to an audience when we design something, what can an interdisciplinary approach help?). We wanted to find a way to incorporate design thinking, which Dam and Siang (2021) define as "an iterative process in which you seek to understand your users, challenge assumptions, redefine problems and create innovative solutions which you can prototype and test," into a rigorous and interdisciplinary curriculum. And we wanted to find a way to teach students how best to capture what the human experience is with any design. This latter goal – measuring the user experience – is where social scientists are particularly adept.

We wrestled with what to call it. We could reference the popular "UX" or user experience design, or cling to a broader focus on "design thinking" or "digital studies." After all, we were trying to find ways to incorporate all of these ideas into our liberal arts approach of critical thinking, interdisciplinarity, and fostering lifelong learning and leadership among our students. Or we could create a name to capture what we really wanted to do: create a program where students would design artifacts or systems (digital or physical or social), and incorporate human responses to those designs in revised iterations of the designs. We ended up proposing an academic program in HCD.

As a sociologist working with colleagues on ways to frame a program in design, I found myself approaching the task as an *applied sociologist* – a person dedicated to solving community problems and issues by using sociological theories and methods to do so (Zevallos 2009). While traditional sociology tends to use similar methods as applied sociology (e.g., surveys, interviews, observations), the motivating force of applied sociology is a client with a particular need rather than the researcher herself. The goal is to meet an immediate practical need, and not necessarily to have the research be vetted by professional peers in an academic publication.

My aims with this book align with the aims of applied sociology, even though I do not have a specific client in mind. Not only do I stress the importance of meeting client and other stakeholder needs as the driving force behind data collection and analysis, I do so with recognition of the importance of ethics, responsibility, inclusion, and the role of the researcher in figuring out who gets included as participants in the project. The book is meant to aid designers and architects who wish to create designs for the good of our social world. Using sociological methods and approaches will help fulfill this wish. And even if some projects result in academic publication of research findings, the primary goal is to more effectively and ethically create designs for those who are engaged with those designs. This situates the book in the field of applied sociology.

The next chapters show what socially-informed research in the design process looks like. I include concrete examples as I detail the steps that highlight social and cultural factors that impact users and their values. I discuss not only ways that sociological concepts and research methods may improve the design process, but also ways that HCD methods and concepts may inform design work (and even sociology itself). And I note how each research step in the design process can help improve future design, leading to a more ethically and sustainably designed world.

Why Does a Pandemic Reveal Timeless Needs for the Integration of Good Data and Good Design?

There's nothing like a pandemic with accompanying lockdowns of schools, workplaces, and places of business to reveal how dependent we are on face-to-face interaction with people who live outside of our own households (and also to reveal that sometimes we can do things virtually that we didn't think were possible). As soon as I found myself limited in terms of locations where I may collect data (no more in-person interviews for a while), and as soon as we bolstered our home's Wi-Fi and rearranged the furniture in our dining room and guest room so my son and I could "go to school" every day, I realized that my sociology and design projects had been drastically changed by our social conditions. The way our social lives and our built environment have been designed and used have been forever changed by COVID-19. Our home and work boundaries are blurred. Our concern for isolation is raised. Our outdoor spaces are reconfigured to function like our living rooms have functioned. Our family and social roles have changed as the economy suffered, jobs were lost, mental health woes were exacerbated (and, in some cases, stabilized to pre-pandemic levels), loved ones fell ill, and schools were closed (and then opened again). We navigated social interaction with face masks and physical distancing (or decided not to include these in some social groups). In the midst of this upheaval, one thing has become apparent: drastic social change reveals the patterns to which we had become accustomed, and provides paths to create new patterns. This is true for design and it is true for the research methods we use to capture data on people's experiences. My hope is that this book can account for these shifts at the same time it can offer timeless tips for data projects associated with design and architecture professions.

Why Is This Book for You?

I have taken on the tall task of writing a book that is meant for an audience that I'm not part of. As a sociologist who speaks to audiences of other social scientists, I can take for granted a collective understanding of some foundational knowledge that I feel compelled to define more clearly here. This is why I have included explicit definitions of terms such as cultural capital, survey, and even ethics in this book. Like any profession, we have our own vocabulary, and speaking with people outside of the profession is an exercise in translation.

Since I'm an outsider to the architecture and design professions (or maybe it would be okay to say I am adjacent to these professions), it may be that some approaches I take in this book with vocabulary, project examples, and participant roles seem unfamiliar or not-quite-accurate to people in these groups, even as architecture and interior design are made up of interdisciplinary bodies of knowledge already. It may seem as if I am conflating the roles of architects and designers (and others), when it is actually the case that these roles are very distinct in terms of education paths, credentials, professional standards, and status within the design world. It may be that the examples I give may not themselves translate across cultural and geographic spaces, even as I advocate for the inclusion of context in any design research. It may be that I omit some practical elements of the design process that seem obvious to architects and designers as central to any research process. In fact, I don't spend much time on cost, materials, and technical processes because those are already covered well in the professions. But of course, considerations of cost, materials, and building permits have to be part of any iterative design process, and often include research elements where stakeholder input is important. Instead of focusing on these things in detail, I delve into social scientific ideas that I think may complement existing knowledge, sometimes at the risk of overgeneralizing or omitting details that people in the trenches would consider first. Because I believe there is a need for greater emphasis on socially-informed research in design, I focus primarily on the social part and the research part. Those are the areas where sociology can be particularly helpful. If at times you find that questions surrounding lighting, permits, and material quality are missing, please don't hesitate to add those into the planning you do for your own projects. You can design an interview or survey project to gather input from end users not only to ask about ways they see a small neighborhood park being more or less likely to promote social interaction in the same set of questions you ask them about how local fire code requirements for engine turnaround space could be incorporated into the design.

I also do not use a lot of terms commonly found in the worlds of business and consulting, in part because that's not my world and in part because there are people who design who are not in these worlds either. People who work in for-profit or not-for-profit work will find utility in the ideas here. I intend the audience of this book to be architects and interior designers, but landscape architects and designers will likely find that their work fits in the approaches I take. Builders and contractors may see themselves as different from the audiences meant for this book, but the tips and ideas presented here are still relevant. In fact, when I chatted with Lynne Jensen-Nelson, a popular public speaker and home building industry training expert, she noted that the key differences between builders and architects/designers relate to scale and professional roles. It is indeed quite different to design and build a custom home for one family than it is to design 1500 new homes with five different floor plans in one market. And the steps of any building process vary in terms of timing and depth of involvement of various stakeholders; it is the builders who carry out the physical manifestation of any design, sometimes long after architects have moved to another project. But builders can learn from socially-informed research practices, too, and I hope they may find utility in some of the ideas presented in this book. Namely, building (like designing) still requires questions about market, end-user and client preferences, builder/designer preferences, cultural and geographic context (and markets), and cost. To illustrate this point, Lynne even noted that the order in which questions are asked of clients (as discussed in Chapter 2) can affect the builder-client relationship (e.g., never ask questions about the budget until you develop a rapport with a client and understand their needs). Architects and designers who produce designs that builders then need to build should consider builders to be key stakeholders in the design process. Builders will produce better buildings, neighborhoods, and communities if they consider the social aspects of the design process and if they are systematic in their approach to gathering input from stakeholders and end users that may inform the building process. After all, if the only driver for building neighborhoods is economic, we would be missing opportunities to infuse socially-informed ideas into projects. Without socially-informed research in any design and building process, the built environment may not be sustainable for present and future communities.

Whether you're a builder, architect, designer, decorator, business owner or head of a non-profit organization with a keen interest in design, I hope you find this book to be useful. You may need to substitute some terminology or examples from your specific profession or work along the way. My examples are meant to be general enough to be able to apply to any of your projects, and specific in terms of the sociologically-informed ideas presented.

Why Keep Reading?

I have written this book in order to offer an efficient set of step-by-step tips and overarching lessons about how to gather useful, meaningful, and socially-informed data about clients' experiences in architecture and interior design professions. I always define terms as I go, and I include vivid and realistic examples from varied professions and at varied scales to illustrate my points, including references to techniques used in varied fields. I include suggestions for how to apply concepts to your own projects. I share stories and anecdotal experiences to humanize the topics. I admit when I am not an expert in a given topic, and bring in the voices of experts in the myriad fields that inform architecture and design projects. I offer tips for additional reading on subjects covered along with examples of real (or realistic) design projects to apply concepts. If you have a particular stage of a project in mind, the chapters are organized so that specific research steps and concepts are easy to bookmark and find again. To this end, I hope this book will serve as a quick reference in your work with individual clients on user studies, and in your ongoing work to tell your data-informed design success stories over time.

While much of what I describe in the book can be done with pen-and-paper or simple computer applications, I do reference some accessible and inexpensive software and methods tools by brand name at times in order to show concretely how projects may look within these kinds of tools. However, I do not provide comprehensive lists or reviews of data products because these references can quickly become outdated as the data tech marketplace rapidly changes and because they may not be accessible to many of the students and professionals who make up the readership for this book.

This Introduction aims to show you why this book matters, and to introduce foundational concepts and framing. The remaining chapters are organized into the big areas that we all think about when we're starting to learn something new: what, how, who, where, when, and (a return to) why. They are also organized in terms of the steps of any research project where data from people is collected, analyzed, and shared. In Chapter 1, I focus on framing a project's goals, research questions, and ethical considerations (the "what"). Chapter 2 covers the "how" – particular research methods available for collecting data. The "who" is covered in Chapter 3, with emphasis on how to involve and communicate with participants (the sample) in the research. In Chapter 4, I cover the "where" and "when" of research, with emphasis on place and time in the research and design process. Chapter 5 (revisiting the "how") continues the research path with coverage of data analysis and presentation for varied audiences. And in the Conclusion, I recap tips for each research step and revisit why socially-informed research matters for architects and interior designers.

In each chapter, I include hypothetical design projects (based on composites of real projects I've worked on) to highlight concepts and methodological steps. I use multiple project examples that cover different institutional realms (e.g., health care sites, schools, residences, eating establishments, museums, theaters). I intersperse large- and small-scale project examples, and both interior design and architecture project examples, not only to show overlaps in these types of projects but also to call attention to differences between those project sizes and professions that may impact the methods used in any given project.

Why should architects and interior designers consider using socially-informed research methods? Why is it important to talk to and learn from those who live/work/play/learn/etc. in our buildings every day? Why is this a necessary step in a holistic design process? Why isn't it enough to assume our assumptions were correct and move on to the next project? I believe that it's not only possible but also crucial to strike a balance between social scientific research methods and concepts and design visions among interior designers and architects. This book is an exercise in translation across these approaches, with the hope that they may inform each other in order to promote more socially sustainable design. Collaboration and social sustainability are key areas of focus in design professions. I offer this book as a way to share sociological tools and ideas with design and architecture professionals to heighten this focus.

If you're interested in using good (and accessible) social scientific methods to gather this information from clients, keep reading. This book contains everything you need to know to enhance your ability to conduct ongoing evaluation of your projects, create useful pre- and post-design evaluations, frame good questions for improved future design, and focus on responsible and evidence-based human-centered design to improve the relationship between socially-informed design and people's lived experiences. It also gives you tools for how to communicate your design success to audiences that include potential clients and other designers.

And so, without further delay, I would like to introduce design to data and data to design and introduce you to both via this *guide to socially-informed research for architects and designers*.

References

Bauman, Zygmut, and Tim May. 2019. *Thinking Sociologically*, 3rd edn. Hoboken, NJ: Wiley-Blackwell.

Beaman, Jean. 2002. "Architectural Sociology." *Footnotes*, December. https://www.asanet.org/sites/default/files/savvy/footnotes/dec02/fn17.html.

Becker, Howard S. 1982. *Art Worlds*. Berkeley: University of California Press.

Bourdieu, Pierre. [1985] 1986. "The Forms of Capital." Pp. 241–258 in *Handbook for Theory and Research for the Sociology of Education*, edited by J. G. Richardson. Westport, CT: Greenwood.

Council for Interior Design. 2020. "Professional Standards 2020." https://static1.squarespace.com/static/5c9ae7530490796e32442342/t/5dd5638d73df8c355b02033f/1574265742484/Professional+Standards+2020.pdf.

Dam, Rikke Friis, and Teo Yu Siang. 2021. "What Is Design Thinking and Why Is It So Popular?" *Interaction Design Foundation*. https://www.interaction-design.org/literature/article/what-is-design-thinking-and-why-is-it-so-popular.

Dam, Rikke Friis, and Teo Yu Siang. 2022. "The History of Design Thinking." *Interaction Design Foundation*, May 17. https://www.interaction-design.org/literature/article/design-thinking-get-a-quick-overview-of-the-history.

Dorris, Jess. 2016. "10 Questions with…Fauzia Khanani." *Interior Design*, February 2. https://interiordesign.net/designwire/10-questions-with-fauzia-khanani/.

Hatleskog, Eli, and Flora Samuel. 2021. "Mapping Social Values." *The Journal of Architecture* 26(1): 56–58.

Hay, Rowena, Flora Samuel, Kelly J. Watson, and Simon Bradbury. 2018. "Post-Occupancy Evaluation in Architecture: Experiences and Perspectives from UK Practice." *Building Research & Information* 46(6): 698–710.

Holland, Oscar. 2022. "Pulitzer Prize 2022: Francis Kéré Becomes First African to Win 'Nobel of Architecture.'" *CNN*, March 15. https://www.cnn.com/style/article/pritzker-prize-2022-francis-kere/index.html.

Janning, Michelle, and Lindsey Menard. 2006. "I Would Never Do That in My Own Home: Audience Reflexivity and the Decorating Television Viewing Culture." *Electronic Journal of Sociology* 10.

Janning, Michelle, and Helen Brambrink (Scalise). 2015. "Gender and Generation in the Home Curation of Family Photography." *Journal of Family Issues* 36(12): 1702–1725.

Janning, Michelle, and Maya Volk. 2017. "Where the Heart Is: Home Space Transitions for Residential College Students." *Children's Geographies* 15(4): 478–490.

Janning, Michelle, Julian Landau, Jess Lilly, Ruby Matthews, and Kaia Roast. 2022. "Coming Home to College: Living Arrangements and Perceptions of Adulthood for U.S. College Students during COVID-19." *Cogent Social Sciences* 8(1): 1–20.

Jones, Bernie. 1984. "Doing Sociology with the Design Professions." *Clinical Sociology Review* 2(1): 109–119.

Lucas, Ray. 2016. *Research Methods for Architecture*. London: Laurence King Publishing.

Mahabadi, Shahab Mirzaean, Hossein Zabihi, and Hamid Majedi. 2014. "Participatory Design: A New Approach to Regenerate the Public Space." *International Journal of Architecture and Urban Development* 4(4): 15–22.

Mills, C. Wright. 1959. *The Sociological Imagination*. London: Oxford University Press.

Nielsen, Jakob. 2000. "Why You Only Need to Test with 5 Users." Nielsen Norman Group, March 18. https://www.nngroup.com/articles/why-you-only-need-to-test-with-5-users/.

Sok, Eloïse. 2018. "Sociology in the Service of Architecture, Or How to Design Comfortable Buildings." Visionary Insights: SageGlass, July 18. https://www.sageglass.com/en/visionary-insights/sociology-service-architecture-or-how-design-comfortable-buildings.

Stevenson, Fionn. 2019. *Housing Fit for Purpose: Performance, Feedback and Learning*. London: RIBA Publishing.

Zevallos, Zuleyka. 2009. "What Is Applied Sociology? A Brief Introduction on Applied Sociology." *Sociology at Work*, May 23. https://sociologyatwork.org/about-2/what-is-applied-sociology/.

Framing a Project's Goals and Research Question – The WHAT

1

I have a box in my office labeled "Awesome Research Projects I Don't Have Time to Do." As someone who has advised hundreds of sociology thesis projects that entail original data collection and analysis, one of my favorite moments in the advising process is when students are just starting to formulate a research question. But before we get to a question, we usually talk about topics that interest them. Whenever a topic comes up that they decide not to do (or whenever a topic comes up that I decide not to pursue in my own research), I jot it down and put it in the box, just in case a future student is seeking ideas for topics. I love this research stage because it offers one of the most creative and fulfilling opportunities to think about where the students' passions lie. Being passionate about a research topic is important because by the time analysis and writing occur, a student will have dedicated the better part of seven months to this labor of love. Being passionate helps my research and it should help any research that occurs in a design project.

What Is the "What?" Defining Data

In any design, data is useful, whether it's MERV air filter ratings, NRC ratings for acoustic tiles, or even wall measurements. Even though these kinds of data are crucial in the design and building or remodeling process, it is also crucial to incorporate data gathered from the people who inhabit or use what is created. Input from people who will engage with the design helps make the design better. This is true regardless of whether the design is new or a revision of a previous design. It is also true regardless of whether the designers and users can identify precisely what problem the design is meant to solve when the project process starts. Socially-informed research in design includes gathering input from people who occupy, inhabit, use, or engage with a design. This input then informs iterations of the design in the hopes that whatever the designer is trying to do (or solve, in the case of an identified problem) will likely succeed and be useful and enjoyable for the users. I refer to this input from users (or inhabitants, or people who occupy a space), in the language of social research as *data*. But, as I elaborate in this chapter, data does not need to be quantitative nor does the gathering of data need to be formal or large scale. It also does not need to be limited to input that people consciously provide. Input from people can take the form of numbers, stories, journals, quick responses to survey questions, observations, and many other forms, elaborated throughout this book. In all of these methods to gather input, an important starting point for any researcher is to ask what constitutes helpful data. This requires a brief interlude about epistemology.

How do you know what you know? This seems like a deeply philosophical question (which, of course, it is), but it's actually pretty straightforward. Think about how you came to know how to design. You probably figured out you had a passion for it at some point, then gained some insights from an educational setting, and then gained experience that then informed your subsequent designs. Similarly, those of us who have a passion for the systematic study of human behaviors and attitudes had a desire to uncover patterns in our social world, then we trained in various methods to notice and write about these patterns, and then we incorporated what we learned from past projects into the future methodological design. In both cases, we know what we know because we were part of a social world where passions may be honed and knowledge may be shared in formal and informal ways. *Epistemology* is a term that refers to all of this: a theory of knowledge that incorporates the position that how we come to know what we know shapes how we approach our projects. In this book, the epistemological approach I use involves systematic collection of empirical data. In other words, this book is meant to teach how to deal with data – how to select, gather, analyze, and write about things we include in our research. And to do so with an epistemological bias toward being careful, systematic, and oriented toward patterns rather than anecdotes or casual one–off observations.

If data is *empirical*, it means it can be verified through observation or experience. If I make a claim that is based on empirical evidence, I am not basing it on suspicion or guesses. Rather, I am basing it on evidence that I have collected from people who use their senses (Can they see it? Hear it? Smell it? Feel it? Taste it?). For sociologists, this usually involves collecting data about human behaviors and attitudes in a systematic way. As subsequent chapters detail, there are myriad ways to be systematic. Sometimes it means quantifying things that are easy to count (e.g., how many people use one doorway as opposed to another). And sometimes it means taking subjective data (e.g., asking people in an open-ended way WHY they use one doorway as opposed to another) and organizing that data into themes, clusters, or patterns that vary from group to group.

Whether the data you collect is quantitative or qualitative, it is possible to use the data to inform future projects. In a sense, this book is really about "data-driven design," but I hesitate to put that phrase in bold because it doesn't fully capture the importance of design itself. In other words, I am a strong advocate for including empirical data gathered from the people who use and inhabit designs, but it is also important to allow for the expertise and innovation of designers themselves to push design ideas forward. Because architects and designers are part of the social world in which the design takes place, and because design should be done in such a way that reduces social inequalities, incorporates social and cultural context, and sustains the natural environment, I advocate for a socially-informed research approach to design.

What Is This Book Not Asking You to Do? Sometimes It's Not about the Data

The title of this book almost included the term "data-driven." I went back and forth about this term. On the one hand, I do not have a problem using the term "data," and I advocate for using data to inform (and even drive) the design process. After all, without systematically gathering information about how people are experiencing a design, designers and architects may repeat mistakes or fail to revise designs as human behaviors and attitudes change. On the other hand, if we fixate too much on occupant data as a driver for design, it may be possible to fall into one of two traps: (1) seeing only the forest and not the trees – relying too much on the shared patterns in the data and not enough on individual stories and (2) being blind to your own vision – losing sight of the importance of designer and architect expertise. I take each of these potential pitfalls in turn. I return to the notion of expertise in Chapter 3.

Seeing Only the Forest and Not the Trees

If we rely too much on group or patterned data that demonstrates the experience and preferences of a majority of users, and not enough on individual stories, we end up putting data-for-its-own-sake on a pedestal and risk making decisions at the expense of exceptional stories, circumstances, or needs – especially of those who cannot access things that able-bodied and well-resourced individuals can. Or, on a pragmatic business level, we wait to make decisions because we don't have a "perfect" dataset, delaying the design process and adding to impatience in clients. By focusing on collective human-centered data, we – perhaps ironically – can lose sight of the human stories that should inform design. It's like seeing only the forest and none of the trees. We may spend so much time assessing the overall pattern of client experience that we forget how much one person's story may actually shape others' experiences and may actually shape future design itself. Socially-informed research, thus, must include mechanisms to distill patterns from the data, and it must allow for the inclusion of individual stories.

Individual experiences with design, even if they do not represent the majority of users, can also end up making things better for everyone. This is an important tenet of *universal design*, which I have seen scholars in education and disability studies define as design that is flexible enough that anyone who engages with the design can find it easy to use and enjoyable, regardless of ability. An example of universal design that I've incorporated into my classroom is making the readings available in hardcopy, audio, and digital formats, thus offering versatility for varied learning modes and adaptability for those whose needs disallow one format or another. In terms of building design for people with vision impairments, the design of an elevator needs to allow for people with and without their eyesight to navigate the doors, buttons, and notifications about what floor they're on. It may seem counterintuitive to suggest that because the design meets the needs of someone with a physical impairment, it meets everyone's needs, especially because people who are not visually impaired do not require revisions to flat elevator buttons or sound clues to note doors opening or closing. But designing an elevator to be inclusive rather than exclusive adheres to values in sustainable design, which, in the long run, benefits everyone. Everyone wins when those with less access have their needs met without taking away the utility for those who don't require this kind of access. In some ways, this is a case of an outlier affecting the overall design. But it's better to think of this as a design based on meeting the needs of everyone regardless of ability. Not only is this a legal issue (as in adhering to the Americans with Disabilities Act), but it is also an ethical one. Just because there is a prevalent pattern does not mean it is the right one to use to inform the design.

But it is not always the case that an individual preference benefits everyone or makes a design better. In some cases, it may lessen the enjoyment or usability for others. Let's say that the lighting was adjusted in an office building because of one person's sensitivity to light (not necessarily due to a visual impairment, but rather just a preference), but then other workers found the lighting to be too dim to complete their work. Whose preference should be accommodated here? Or, let's say that in a home remodel, a client tells a vivid story about a childhood memory attached to the color purple, which leads a designer to infuse purple in some small way in every room. But this is a color that the other household residents despise. Whose preference should be accommodated here? These examples show that individual stories may not represent a larger pattern but do impact future design and user experiences and may lead to problematic design decisions (or designs that lead to conflict among those who use the spaces). Sometimes these individual ideas and needs make our designs more universally helpful (better access to clear elevator features is good for everyone), and sometimes they are more focused on one person's needs that may not be useful for everyone (beware the dangers of dim lighting or too much purple). It is important to be able to tell the difference between these two possible outcomes so that we find the right balance of individual and collective stories. Sometimes this takes the form of a designer choosing the option that meets most people's needs while including small elements that allow for flexibility for individual people who have unique needs or preferences. Maybe one room is purple, or changeable purple fabric is used instead of permanent wall color. Maybe a creative use of shades and strategically placed lamps could help the person who prefers less bright office lighting. In order to discern how much to pay attention to individual versus majority preferences, a designer needs to know what kinds of questions to ask people to reach a decision or compromise.

Being Blind to Your Own Vision

What if the "outlier" in the preferences expressed during the design process is the designer? For anyone in a design profession, talking with a client is always a delicate balance of meeting their desires alongside your beliefs about what constitutes good design and your knowledge of what is actually possible to build or buy. If you focus too much on gathering input from those who dwell in your designs, you may lose sight of the fact that people do not always know how to reflect on whether a design is working for them, that people have a hard time focusing on future needs because attitudes are based on past experience, and that the design itself may be good even if people have not found a way to situate themselves in it. I've seen this in numerous interactions between architects and clients. The conversation often goes like this:

Architect to participants: What do you think of the design of this space? Does it meet the goal you articulated of creating safe and inviting interactional moments for residents?

PARTICIPANT 1: I think green chairs are uninviting, and what I'd really like to see is a big trapeze set in the foyer.

ARCHITECT (in their own head): Must. Be. Patient. Color is not what I'm asking about here, and we already settled on green in a previous input session. But I'll note this in case others agree that color matters for creating a safe and inviting space. Also, I am not able to defy the laws of physics in this design.

ARCHITECT (out loud): Thanks for this input. What do others think?

Buildings, furniture, and fixtures seem like static entities in our lives, when actually our built environment and objects are often more dynamic. Our spaces are settings in which changing social lives, roles, and activities take place. We are pretty good at adapting to spaces that may have been designed for people who are not like us, or for a different era, or for a different activity. But even though we adapt to our spaces, it is crucial to design new spaces that are the "best attempts" to allow for flexible use as our world and its inhabitants change. And we should probably avoid adding a trapeze to most designs.

Architects and designers have an eye for the future, designing spaces and objects that move us forward – often at a faster pace than the people who use the designs. Sometimes it takes people using a design to know that it is good, adaptable, or long-lasting. The capacity to see the beauty and efficacy (and technical requirements) of design before others can should not be ignored even as data about client views and behaviors inform future design. Informing future design should consist of a balance between expertise in terms of aesthetic choices and technical knowledge and people's use and views of the space. An over-reliance on either can result in good design that is never used (which arguably is not good design) or used spaces that don't adhere to high standards in design.

Importantly, sometimes designing for its own sake, which leads to form taking precedence over function, can result in problems. Some architecture and design programs include studio assignments that, when aggregated, allow students to create a portfolio of innovative designs where the visual representation of those designs is the primary focus at the expense of practical matters (e.g., a beautifully rendered 3-D model of an office design with all of the latest innovations in technology and aesthetic trends with no spaces dedicated to toilets). While the designer's talent and capacity to visibly render the design in a beautiful way is showcased, the problem with this is that stakeholders and eventual users of the design will not be able to picture themselves in the space. Beautiful design is great, but if there's no bathroom, everyone will be too distracted to notice. So, design is always about balancing ego and accepting critique; form and function; beautiful and usable. In architecture and design school, taking advantage of critique sessions can help students be able to capture the voice of stakeholders who may inhabit the design in their eventual design practices. This is good for business, to be sure. But it's also good for our social world, where meeting people's diverse needs must be part of good design.

The purpose of this book is to help you learn how to gather and interpret information from the people who use and live in your designs. This requires some skills in recognizing patterns that may gloss over idiosyncratic experiences. It requires looking through an objective lens at subjective experiences. But it does not require being fixated on data for its own sake. In my own work, I rely on data and stories. The trick is to discern when to make decisions based on the patterns that data from lots of people reveal, and when to make decisions based on a good story that, if retold well, can actually reflect important patterns.

What Type of Project, Type of Variables, and Type of Data Make Sense?

The type, size, location, and level of complexity of any design projects conducted by readers of this book are likely as varied as the design aesthetics themselves. Some of you may work as architects or designers in large firms, often designing with a team dedicated to all the complexities of a big building project. Some of you may be part of a smaller operation, or perhaps you work on your own as an interior designer. You may work in an urban or rural setting, in US-based locales, or across the globe. Or you may be designing a new large hospital but figure out that talking with just a few people about a small area such as a reception desk may suffice for gathering helpful input. Gathering input to inform design can happen no matter the size of the space and size of the group of stakeholders who will use that space. My hope is to present strategies for decision-making about data that transcend size of firm or team, type of design, scope of project, location, or cost of all of this. At the same time, I also discuss ways that project variation along these factors may matter in the research processes.

When thinking about what to study, it is important to consider time. While Chapter 4 delves deeply into the importance of time and sequence in any socially-informed research that is part of the design process, suffice it to say now that data used to inform design looks a bit different if done before, during, or after the design process is completed. More specifically, what you research before you know any needs of your design's users looks different than how their experiences look after the design is done. Pre-test research topics can be different from post-occupancy evaluations, even as they may include topics that are researched at every design stage.

Earlier I defined empirical data to be things that are observable or experienced, and I noted that I approach data in a systematic, rather than haphazard or anecdotal, way. Researchers decide which type of data to collect based on many factors. One such factor in sociological research is the *unit of analysis*: the size of the entity – individual or group – that, when collected or aggregated, makes up a sample being studied. Necessarily, all data collected about human behaviors and attitudes can be boiled down to individual-level data. Even massive datasets capturing GDP or national happiness indexes include individuals in the datasets. But sometimes the angle we take in our research organizes the sample into groups rather than individuals as we move from data collection to data analysis.

Allow me to explain using examples. Imagine that you want to assess whether a particular seating arrangement works well for encouraging conversation among small groups of people. If you were interested in this topic for individual homeowners remodeling their living rooms, it would make sense to use the individual as a unit of analysis, perhaps through one-on-one interviews or observations of their behaviors in mock-ups of the design. But as soon as you scale the project to compare different arrangements of furniture in spaces with varied levels of openness across two organizations, it may make more sense to think about the dataset as consisting of groups or constituencies, rather than just a collection of individuals. In the case of a multi-organization or multi-space design project, your unit of analysis may be groups: office staff in organization A and office staff in organization B. You may even divide the groups further to differentiate between workers who are part-time or full-time, or who have varied arrangements in terms of working remotely. In any case, whether you gather individual-level data one user at a time (collected over time and across multiple small projects) or group-level data in clusters of people all at once (which could be collected at multiple stages in a design process), your unit of analysis needs to help you answer your research question.

The unit of analysis matters especially if you are collecting data from a group all at once or collecting data from individuals one-at-a-time. One-at-a-time user data may be required either because your designs are small-scale with individual users (one or very few for each design, as with a series of home remodels), or because the needs of a large-scale project vary by small group within the larger user group (as with a school remodel meant to meet highly variable learning needs of small groups of students).

A research question not only needs to be answered using the right unit of analysis (individuals or groups), but it also needs to be phrased in such a way that the factors you want to study are easy to actually transform into studyable topics. This requires transforming factors that are abstract into variables that can be measured. A *variable* is a characteristic that varies from unit of analysis to unit of analysis. All variables need to be operationalized. *Operationalization* is the process of changing an abstract concept into a measurable variable. Put in simpler terms, a variable is a feature or factor that changes "scores" from person to person or group to group. Creating a full list of possible scores for that variable is operationalization. For example, at an individual level, favorite color may be a variable. One easy way to operationalize this variable is simply to ask people what their favorite color is, and then provide a list of many colors from which people can choose their favorite. Normally in sociology we refer to the "scores" along a variable (such as green or blue or purple for favorite color) as *attributes*.

Other variable examples include annual income, preferred design style, or even what neighborhood you live in. These are all characteristics that can vary from person to person (even if it's hard to think about someone "scoring" a particular design style). These are all traits that change at an individual level.

But what about groups? If it is important to conduct socially-informed research in the design process, how should we think about variable operationalization at the group level? For example, while knowing individual incomes for clients in a specific neighborhood can help us see what they are able to afford, it can also be helpful to know the average annual income in one neighborhood compared to another neighborhood in order to assess what kinds of home designs may be more or less typical. Average annual income by neighborhood is a variable that is calculated using individual incomes (and then taking an average), but the use of this as a way to compare neighborhoods means that income is also measured using groups (the neighborhood) as the unit of analysis.

To illustrate variable operationalization related more closely to design, let's say an organization has hired a design firm to redesign a work space to be more conducive to collaboration. A primary research question guiding the redesign of an office space is whether increasing the level of physical openness in work space increases the level of collaboration. Here are examples of variables that could be used that require measurement using the individual as the unit of analysis for this kind of project (with a brief note about possible methods that could be used to gather data, which is elaborated in Chapter 2):

- Likelihood of using the open spaces more than in the past to perform work tasks (which could be assessed by asking individuals to keep a record or journal of their work locations over time, both before and after a redesign)
- Level of desire to collaborate more with others before and after increased openness in the work space (which could be assessed by interviewing or surveying individual people about their attitudes before and after a redesign)

These are variables that can vary from person to person, and it makes sense to gather individual-level data, even if the ultimate goal is to tabulate all of the individual results to note any overall patterns (e.g., people collaborate more and spend more time in open vs private areas, which may mean the new design is fostering more collaboration). In fact, these variables seem to be quite psychological in nature (preference for spaces, desire for types of work experiences). But it is possible and important to think of these topics as variables that may be operating at the group level more explicitly, especially because patterns that are occurring at the organizational level may be easier to see. It is also possible to note changes from group to group even as the data that is gathered starts at the individual level. Pay attention to how the phrasing of the topics changes when the unit of analysis moves from individual to group:

- Likelihood of tech-focused teams to use open spaces more than closed spaces for their team tasks (which could be assessed by observing specific groups' behaviors)
- Proportion of team projects that are collaborative before and after the increase in open spaces in the workplace (which could be assessed by identifying a full list of projects as more or less collaborative and calculating proportions within total number of projects)

In order to perform socially-informed research, it is necessary to set up research questions with variables that ultimately will allow for group-level data to be collected. Sometimes starting with groups as the unit of analysis is required. To be socially-informed means that factors such as group membership, level of access to resources, and cultural context can all shape individuals' experiences and attitudes. Thus, even if you don't spend time wrestling with figuring out whether a variable is measured using an individual or group unit of analysis, your focus should be on group patterns. After all, a workplace or any built environment is not simply a collection of individuals. It is a place where groups and networks impact type of activity, level of access to resources such as money, time, and space, and values about privacy and collaborative work.

Once you know what you'd like to measure, it helps to think ahead to data analysis in terms of what *level of measurement* each variable is. Level of measurement is another way to classify variables by type – in this case, whether the variable is a category, a ranking, or a number where a mathematical mean can be calculated. Some variables are really only about categories, where the answer choices (or attributes) are not really ranked, and where the "scores" of people in your sample (when added up) really only tell you how many people choose particular answers (not, say, what the average score on a scale of 1 to 5 is). This level of measurement is *nominal or categorical*. For example, let's say you want to assess people's emotional response to a particular color palette for a foyer. You could ask people what color palette they prefer from among a set of three. Your data analysis would then consist of counting the number of people who chose each color palette, perhaps going with the one that was most popular. For individuals participating in your research, they're not answering with numbers. They are choosing a category where the full list of categories is not really in a rank order as it's presented to them. This is nominal or categorical data.

What if you want to see how individual people may rank a set of choices? Instead of asking which one people prefer the most, you could ask them to rank their preferences from among the three choices by using a scale of 1 to 3 or by using image-based rankings such as gold, silver, and bronze medals, or even facial expressions as we see in pain scales hanging in medical clinics. If you do this, you have turned your nominal variable into an *ordinal variable*, where the attributes are ranked, but not necessarily numeric. Examples of this in survey research include questions where people are asked to rate their level of agreement with a statement, rate something on a numeric or sliding scale, or give a certain number of stars in a review. An ordinal variable, like a nominal or categorical variable, is not necessarily something where you'd calculate a mathematically meaningful mean for your sample (though you could), but where you could see which foyer color palette has the most #1's, gold medals, or smiley faces.

For variables where a mean or median will be used in analyses where statistical significance tests are used, and where we assess the numeric responses using the principles of the central limit theorem and probability theory, an *interval-ratio variable* can be used. These are variables where the attributes (or possible answers) are numbers. An example of this includes the number of times people take a certain path within a foyer. A note about statistical significance tests, especially if the terms "central limit theorem" and "probability theory" make your head spin: if you find yourself wanting to conduct analyses using correlations, regression, or other techniques, you can do these using ordinal data if that data is turned into numbers (e.g., change the gold medal to 1, silver to 2, and bronze to 3, and then calculate a mean for the group). In social science research, we do this often. Technically it violates the rules of statistics to do this, but it is not uncommon. If you do this, you have to be careful to note that the data may violate some of these rules. But calculating a mean for ordinal variables and then comparing group means using a significance test such as a *t*-test or analysis of variance (ANOVA) can still tell you whether the differences between groups are likely real differences or simply due to chance. By the way, I do not go into detail here about statistical significance tests; if you're interested in using these, you may want to take a course in statistics. For most socially-informed research in the design process, you won't need this level of statistical sophistication. When working with a client or end-users, it is often good enough to say "a majority of stakeholder group A preferred X, whereas most of group B preferred Y."

In sum, using nominal, ordinal, or interval-ratio data in your research will result in different types of analysis and reporting of findings. As you think through your variable operationalization, think ahead to how it may most help your project in the reporting by asking these questions related to level of measurement: Do I need numbers of people who prefer or do something? Do I need people's numeric preferences or number of times for a particular action that could result in a group mean? Do I just need ideas for the categories of things that people prefer or do? Would it be helpful to show how individual people rank choices (which requires ordinal or interval-ratio variables) or would it suffice to show how the group as a whole shows preference for certain categories where each person only chose one preference (which nominal variables can provide)?

One more note about how best to define variables and how best to think about data: When I've set up data projects for organizations who think that they may be incapable of coming up with (let alone measuring) variables or gathering useful data, I begin with these four questions about data:

- Is it meaningful?
- Is it measurable?

- Is it accessible?
- Is it trackable over time?

As you think about ways to capture people's experiences and attitudes with your design, always ask these questions. Even if you are doing a *cross-sectional* project (one snapshot in time, rather than *longitudinal*, in which the research tracks data over time) with only one client, including variables that could be used in each design project after this would allow for you to track design impact over time. Even if you have access to a lot of data for a larger project, be sure to check that the data that you'd use to assess whether the design is working should be meaningful (just because you have data doesn't mean you should use it). Even if you find the best way to measure users' experiences, you have to be able to have access to those users in the first place. And even if your projects consist of a collection of stories and anecdotes, you should be able to find patterns that can inform current and future designs.

At the beginning of this section, I noted that I hoped the ideas presented here would be applicable to any design project, regardless of project size, scale, or unit of analysis. However, these factors do shape how we should be thinking about data. Your research questions will differ depending on whether you are working with a large design team on a multi-phase multi-million dollar project where thousands of people will be inhabiting the design, or on a single-family home being remodeled to adapt to a physically disabled family member. But regardless of the scale of the project, the focus on individuals or groups as the unit of analysis (and the level of measurement of your variables) needs to be figured out before data is collected. And, whenever possible, the data you collect and analyze should be meaningful, measurable, accessible, and trackable over time.

What Is a Good Research Question?

Architecture scholar Ray Lucas (2016) says that defining a research question is basically figuring out the answer to the question "What do you want to find out?" (25). Lucas elaborates that in architectural research, the question may be given to you by a client, or you may be trying to fill in a gap or remedy a deficiency in the existing research in your field. While enhancing the body of knowledge within architecture and design research is a great goal (and is discussed further in Chapter 5), the focus of this book is to teach you how to come up with a research question that can be used in multiple situations in architecture and design practice. Because of this, the goals of any design project are first and foremost centered on the client's wishes and needs. But this doesn't mean that you can't ask a research question that can benefit people who engage with your designs (and those of others) in the future; nor does it mean that your research can't add to existing knowledge in the field.

Studying how users actually use a space requires asking the right questions to assess this use. Imagine a client asking for a design that meets the needs of building occupants who have challenges with physical mobility and vision. Throughout the design process, a good designer will make sure the user data collected includes measures that capture the success or failure of the design in meeting mobility and vision needs. Are visual cues that align with the aesthetics of a space clearly marked and available in non-visual mediums? Can people who walk at varied paces or who use assistive devices navigate moving from one floor to another? Can everyone reach buttons and find directions so they know where to go? Would any of these needs lead to incompatible design elements?

But in this example, the term "needs" is worth unpacking a bit. Certainly, there are physical aspects of design that allow or disallow different types of bodies from accessing or enjoying spaces. It is easy to see these as needs. But importantly, building a ramp or offering directions in braille are not universally enacted, nor were they enacted much in the US until recent decades. Needs, and the capacity of designers to meet those needs, vary across space and time.

Beyond the historical transformation of accessibility laws and norms, it is also the case that needs have come to include responses from users that are often invisible or not physical. Often these come in the form of subjective and psychological responses. For example, assistive devices for mobility may not be needed by people who have no mobility limitations, but seeing these in a building may make them believe the organization values universal design and accessibility. Beyond the individual, we also ought to consider how social needs are met, and what created our understanding of these needs in the first place. Varying levels of adherence to inclusion, community, and privacy? All socially created. All important. All possible to include in any sociological study of user experience of design where the research question is "are everyone's vision and mobility needs met?" But this is a tall order. Let's break down the creation of a research question a bit more.

In our sociology program, we require all senior undergraduate students to write a thesis wherein they pose a question, review literature, apply theoretical lenses, gather and analyze data, present findings, and offer interpretation and implications of those findings using past research and theory as a way to frame their interpretation. Before they start their thesis research, we spend a couple of weeks doing exercises that move from interest to topic to question. It can be daunting to know that countless topics can be the focus of thesis research in sociology, so we work on funneling it down to make it more doable (Booth et al. 2016). For designers conducting socially-informed research, the process is the same.

In class, we have students fill in this sentence: I am studying _____ because I want to find out who/what/when/where/whether _____ in order to _____. When you ask a question that is meant to get at the experience of those who inhabit your designs, it is helpful to ask whether your aim is to *describe* their experience or to *explain* it.

Description and explanation are both helpful approaches, but they have different outcomes. To describe something means to detail things such as color, brightness, physical layout, patterns of flow from space to space, what era the design may reference, which people are present in various spaces within a larger design, and where a design is situated in reference to a larger space. Descriptive research gets at what, who, where, and when (despite this chapter's focus on the "what," these are all helpful terms to understand the kinds of things designers can pay attention to in descriptive analysis). Sometimes it can also get at how, as in how people move from one space to another (in terms of traffic flow, use of particular paths, with or without barriers). In a new playground design, useful descriptive research questions could include: What kinds of children and families are using this in terms of age, racial-ethnic identity, and gender? What times of day is the playground most used? What activities yield the most frequent use from children? How are children using the equipment besides its intended use? If the playground design is meant to replace an existing structure, you could also ask these same descriptive questions before designing a new one so that post-design evaluation can include comparisons across the same exact factors.

In addition to knowing the what, who, when, where, and how about a space, it is important to move to WHY, which is central to explanatory research. This is the "in order to _____" section of the exercise noted above. If a neighborhood association approached you to design a new playground, you would likely gather descriptive data as suggested above. But you'd also likely want to know why a particular design may be better than another, or why a replacement playground is needed in the first place. Why is there a low turnout of children and families to this playground? Once a new one is designed and you notice differences in use among groups, you may want to understand why this difference is happening. If the goal is to create different spaces for different groups, then you can see the design as successful. If the goal is to create spaces that allow for any group to feel comfortable, then you'd use the answer to the "why" question to amend the design before the playground gets built. For example, let's say you want the playground to foster interaction across age groups because you understand that this facilitates positive socialization. You base this assertion on past research about building empathy in children, which also may enhance neighborhood and community connections. Once you pilot or prototype a design that is intended to allow for integration across ages, you observe use to see if your goal is met. If it is not met, you would then ask why again. Maybe the design incorporates too many age-specific symbols that older kids shy away from. Or maybe there is something besides a playground design that could explain why ten-year-olds are not playing with four-year-olds. This understanding may lead you to reconsider the design so that you could offer options that are more about different ages enjoying some part of the playground rather than all ages enjoying all of it. Of course, this example also carries with it the obvious design decisions about safety, body size, and physical abilities that vary by age for children, but the deeper question of why kids do certain things warrants more than observation of just descriptive data.

Perhaps the greatest gifts we can get from good explanatory research are predictability and further knowledge about design's ongoing capacity to meet human needs and desires. Once a playground designer has been able to incorporate the who, what, when, where, how, and why into a design, they can more easily design future playgrounds with confidence, and they can more easily talk with future clients about the good outcomes of their designs. This makes their design evidence-based. It works especially well when the designer poses the right questions to assess whether a design will work, when the designer can fill in the blanks when studying _____ to find out who/ what/when/where/whether _____ in order to _____.

It is precisely this kind of work that is the focus of architecture scholar Christina Bollo (2021), who frames the importance of *feed-forward design*. Perhaps you have heard of a feedback loop – where user experience with a design is incorporated by the designer who goes "back to the drawing board" to revise the design. With teaching, this can also occur in the process of teaching a concept, finding a way to assess whether students understand or can apply that concept, and then using that set of learning outcomes to inform ongoing teaching to ensure student learning is improved as the semester progresses.

The use of the term "feed forward" by Bollo, however, speaks to the inherent problem of design: you can't easily redesign a building once it's built. Much to some clients' dismay, a redo is likely not possible. During the design process, the hope is to build in enough feedback mechanisms so that the final design works well. What Bollo offers is that, even if a design does not fully meet the needs of clients in that iteration, the designer will incorporate ideas learned in the process in order to feed into future designs. You learn that a design from five years ago didn't work as well as you'd hoped in terms of frequency of use, so you use feedback from that design to design a new building that better meets that need moving forward. The reason this is helpful for any client to understand (even ones who may not think a design turned out exactly as they had hoped) is that your inclusion of this thoughtful and explicit process in your work can instill confidence in you by your future clients. It is this model that inspires innovation, prevents over-promising to clients, and allows you to promise that the voices of current users or residents can inform not just their building, but the next design, too.

Your design portfolio is thus not a static collection of one-and-done designs; rather it is an animated sequence of designs that inform each other and that create iterative improvements. This is not to say that past designs are inherently worse than present ones (I can say that some of my past work outshines some current projects, for example). Rather, as you encounter new clients who want to have confidence in their architect or designer, it is helpful to show how design is a process rather than a product. It is helpful to convey that your experience informs your work, just as their experience informs their engagement with your design. If you inform them that you have incorporated systematic input from people all along, you will also instill trust in any new clients.

Bollo also notes that feed-forward design fosters collaboration among designers, architects, and academicians who study architecture and design. Aside from an abstract understanding of the difference between descriptive and explanatory questions, designers and architects also come to rely on past knowledge and practice to preemptively answer some of the who, what, where, when, how, and why questions. Past designs can also help us see which questions matter the most given particular locations, populations, or goals. Past knowledge gained from other design professionals can inform the current design and the questions chosen to assess that design. And, if I may offer, past knowledge in sociology about people's behaviors that move beyond a psychological interpretation of their lives can also be helpful.

The process of incorporating past ideas (from yourself or from others) into current design operates a lot like writing a literature review in a scientific paper. A *literature review* is a brief summary of past research organized into themes, all of which justify the importance of a question, offer a reader background information to understand all of the factors that go into the question, and point to places where the research may be missing new or better data. One of my favorite analogies for a literature review is a pub. Imagine that you walk into a neighborhood pub in a new city in order to find out what the best things to do for fun are in that city. You notice several tables, all with people discussing different topics and ideas. If you go from table to table, you'd notice that each has people making claims about this activity or that one, perhaps even disagreeing. The table by the window is discussing arts activities; the table by the bar is discussing sporting activities; the table in the corner is focused on activities to do with young children. It would behoove you to capture a bit about what the big ideas and tips are from each table in order to digest what is already known about city fun. It would also behoove you to visit all the tables, because you may realize that nobody at any table is talking about a very important topic: what architectural styles are present in the city. That, then, becomes the focus of your research. But you wouldn't be able to make the bold claim that – despite a lot of existing knowledge out there about city fun – nobody has fully answered the question unless you assessed what is already known. You can't discover something new unless you know what's already been discovered.

Even if you don't conduct a formal literature review (in a pub or elsewhere), design can work the same way. When you design a space, inevitably you are informed by your past research and practice on what works and what doesn't work. This may be formal academic research, or it may be based on the experience you've gathered. Either way, you know the body of knowledge (including sub-bodies) that supports your design decisions. And you also may know what questions remain unanswered.

In Chapter 5, I discuss how to analyze data and tell the data story. In other words, I share ideas for how to (a) know what the answer to your research question is, (b) share it with others, and (c) use it to inform future design. But knowing how to set up a good research question in the first place will make data analysis better. And in order to set up a good project with a good research question, you need to know what different answers to that question will mean in terms of knowing whether the design goals worked or not. If your research question is whether people are comfortable working in a new open-concept work space, for example, you need to know the following:

- What you mean by comfort (variable)
- How to measure it (operationalization) and at what level of measurement
- Whether to focus on individual or group experiences (unit of analysis)
- What would constitute an answer to your research question

The last point requires knowing whether getting a certain proportion of people saying "it's very comfortable" is enough for you to say the design worked. It is therefore helpful to establish benchmarks or thresholds before you collect data. You can base these benchmarks on different things, depending on the aims of your research. Maybe it's a comparison between past and present (an improvement, hopefully). Maybe it's a comparison between one group and another (more comfortable in this organization as opposed to that one). Maybe it's a comparison to some sort of external standard or ideal (more comfortable than the industry standards or best practices).

In addition to figuring out what would constitute a certain answer to your research question before you collect data, it is also important to decide how fancy you want to be with your analysis. If you are inclined to use sophisticated statistical significance tests to understand the impact of your design, you will need to formulate a question that includes variables that can be operationalized and included in these kinds of analyses. If you are inclined to collect a small number of user stories, you will need to think about how many stories may be required to answer your question. Analytic techniques and sample deliberations are elaborated in later chapters.

What Are the Best Ways to Set Up Data Files and Storage Systems?

As I started writing this book, I found myself glancing periodically at my Trello page, which is the online project management platform I was using to keep track of progress on various sections and writing steps. Today I'm alternating screens between this manuscript and the Google sheet where I'm tracking word counts (complete with a formula that automatically adds whatever I list for today's word count to the total count). I realized that Trello was not working as well for me at keeping track of progress in terms of chapter lengths for this particular project, so I switched systems halfway through writing. Switching meant that I also needed to spend half a day setting up a new tracking system for writing progress, but it was worth it.

Part of the process of writing for me has included setting up a system to store files (chapters, sources, notes) and keep track of progress. Trello was recommended to me by an interior designer friend who uses it for her design projects. And spreadsheets are familiar to me in my work as a social scientist. All of my book projects have included a project management process that I set up that includes some sort of design element (e.g., decorative paper and clips moved across a "ruler" to note progress; magnetic paper that I slid from left to right on a large wall to capture completion; an online system with colors and images that symbolize type of project and steps within projects; color-coded columns and word count tracking on a spreadsheet). I have also seen these kinds of tools in the form of Kanban boards and other systems that organizations and individuals use to monitor progress (and feel good about it along the way).

When you conduct a design project (whether it involves research or not), it is helpful to use a system to keep track of progress – one that makes sense to you, one that includes concrete and visible markers of progress, and one that can be accessed quickly and easily to share that progress with collaborators.

So, what elements go into a system like this? File or project element names and aesthetics matter. Yes, what you name files and how they look in any project management platform are worth thinking about and designing before you begin. This means deciding what to name a spreadsheet with client data in it (and how best to keep it confidential and secure, if there is private information in it), or how to ensure you know which file is the most recent iteration (don't make the mistake I used to make, which was labeling a file "Final Edits" before I was actually done editing). Often this means including dates in the file name so you quickly know which one is the most recent. Know if alpha-numeric organization of files works for you, or if some other method works better. Set up folders even if there are no files in them to start. If you change a file name in one place, immediately change it in others. In digital or physical project management platforms, use color or helpful images to organize types of files. If you use varied platforms for the project (e.g., a physical and digital tablet), build in ways to transfer them into a singular storage system so the format of files doesn't distract you from the content. And back up your files. Most importantly, allow time within the design process itself to attend to file management, and to record progress. What happens behind the scenes of any project matters for the success of the project, even if it is not as immediately gratifying or visible to others.

One final note: In a sense, as I revised my writing progress tracking tools, I was incorporating human-centered design into the design of my book project. Even though I was the only person in the sample of users, I assessed how my experience was going, figured out it wasn't working, and used that figuring to inform a redesign. I switched tracking systems after I systematically assessed how the previous system was not meeting my needs.

What Ethical Considerations Matter When Setting Up a Project?

Gathering input from people who inhabit your designs is not just an empirical project, it is also an ethical one. *Research ethics* – the formal and informal rules we use to ensure that we are conducting our research legally, compassionately, and justly – need to guide socially-informed research. Entire books have been written about social research ethics and research organizations have their own ethics codes, including the American Sociological Association (https://www.asanet.org/sites/default/files/asa_code_of_ethics-june2018a.pdf) and the Association for Applied and Clinical Sociology (https://www.aacsnet.net/4108-2/), but I'm only briefly discussing the key points here that stem from my experience as a sociologist working with designers and architects. Throughout this book, each project example and tip are offered with a goal of abiding by high ethical standards for social researchers, and Chapter 3 elaborates on ethics when thinking about research as a set of relationships with other people. Here I wish to point out that in order to create a socially sustainable design to meet the needs of users, we need to ask not only what feels right to us but also what feels right to people participating in our research.

Every stage of the research process contains ethical considerations. As we formulate research questions, we need to be careful not to let our own biases steer the framing of the question. If our clients are paying us, we need to think about what is motivating us – making them happy so we get paid or making sure their needs are met so that they enjoy the design (which also means we get paid)?

As we design the data collection process, we need to think about whether we'll keep people's identities confidential or not (and inform them of this). We also need to understand the difference between confidentiality and anonymity. *Confidentiality* means that we know who the participants in the research are (as when we do face-to-face interviews), but we don't disclose their identities to others outside of the project. On the other hand, *anonymity* (often possible with online surveys of large groups of people where individual IP addresses are removed) means we don't know the specific identities of people who participate in the research.

We need to make sure people who agree to participate in the research understand where and how the results will be used or shared. If the project is meant to produce data that could be used in an academic research article or book to make claims about generalized knowledge, likely the designer is affiliated with a university or organization that would require a formal human subjects or ethics review, often in the form of an Institutional Review Board. But even for people designing for one client at a time with no desire to publish the results beyond internal sharing, informing people about how their input will be used is important. Transparency about how input is used in the design process (and in future designs) is necessary in order for people to trust the design process. In fact, without transparency and trust, some groups of people are disinclined to participate in research in the first place, especially if they are part of groups where research itself has caused harm. This matters, in particular, for people of color in the US, who have been part of medical and social research that has been conducted without informed consent, and that has resulted in physical and psychological trauma for participants (see, e.g., a synopsis of the unethical Tuskegee syphilis study for more information, at https://www.cdc.gov/tuskegee/timeline.htm).

Finally, ethics matter in how data is used and shared. Accurate calculations, adherence to high standards in data analytic techniques, and giving credit to other people when ideas are not our own are all ethical practices. Whether the results of a socially-informed research project are shared with clients, with users, with colleagues in an architecture or design firm, or with professional peers at a conference, accuracy about data is not only more honest, but it better captures the reality of how people are engaging with the design. High ethical standards are required in socially-informed research, and designs will be more socially sustainable as a result.

References

Bollo, Christina. 2021. "The Measure of Success." Paper presented at the American Institute of Architects National Housing Awards (online). May 3. https://network.aia.org/viewdocument/aia-national-housing-awards?CommunityKey=3934f0d4-c0c1-4600-b8a2-844131ba8365&tab=librarydocuments.

Booth, Wayne C., Gregory G. Colomb, Joseph M. Williams, Joseph Bizup, and Wililam T. Fitzgerald. 2016. *The Craft of Research*, 4th edn. Chicago, IL: University of Chicago Press.

Lucas, Ray. 2016. *Research Methods for Architecture*. London: Laurence King Publishing.

Choosing a Research Method to Inform Design – The HOW

2

When I advise students in the development of their sociological research projects, they often start with a method in mind, either because they feel confident or excited about one method more than another (I've always wanted to do in-person interviews!), or because they are concerned with the timing and logistics of data collection (I don't have time to transcribe all those interviews!). Both of these reasons are legitimate, since we have to be realistic about our comfort level with certain ways to gather data, and we have to consider any time or resource constraints. While we may think that doing a rigorous scientific survey with a sample of 2,000 people or a small in-depth interview study of 15 people will give us the best results, either of these may be a tall order depending on our comfort and resources.

Conducting any type of research may be a tall order if the method does not fit with the question. To me, it is always better to start with the development of a question and then move to the data collection method that best helps us answer that question, rather than the other way around. Or at least we should be open to methods and research questions informing each other throughout the design process.

Unless every design you do is the same and is meant for the same use and clientele, it will be helpful for you to vary your data collection method as you vary your designs, questions, and clientele. In Chapter 1, I introduced ways to come up with a good question. In this chapter, I delve into strategies for choosing the best method to answer a question.

How Should You Gather Data? Customer Satisfaction Surveys and Design Drawings in the Staff Break Room May Not Be Enough

Think about the following scenarios:

1. A team of architects and interior designers have been hired to make better use of an empty lot next to an office building, perhaps by creating a park or amphitheater. They want to assess not only what people in the building may want, but also what community members who may use the place in the future may think. The team wonders if it would be better to watch what people do in a nearby park, ask office workers what they'd like to do in the new park, or some combination of these methods. They also wonder at what stage a mock-up of the park (and perhaps amphitheater) should be shown to the community, and where it should be placed for people to engage with it.
2. A team of architects and designers is hired to redesign airports in two countries with varied norms about physical distancing (pre- and post-COVID-19). They want to compare what people are doing now and set up future data collection to anticipate changing rules and norms. They also want to compare and contrast what people do in the two locations. They wonder if interviewing airport staff members and observing passengers will give them useful data.
3. An interior designer wants to expand his clientele to include the population of 65+ individuals who are deliberating about whether to "age in place" or live in a collective housing location with various lifestyle and health-assistance amenities. He wonders if people in this age category may be more comfortable sitting down in groups or individually to talk about their wants and needs, or if observation of what they're currently doing would suffice.

When we craft a research question as social scientists, an accompanying step in the research process is to figure out which data is best to gather to answer the question and how best to gather that data. The same is true in architecture and design projects where a problem needs to be solved or question answered. Should we ask people questions or just watch them use a space? Should we seek their input in face-to-face conversations or give them the option to write down ideas in private? Should we allow for input to be collected as part of a hands-on trial or simulation or ask mostly hypothetical questions?

There are myriad options for what kind of data to use and how to get the data. This section outlines many of those options, both generally and specifically. Whatever method you choose should give you the right kind of evidence needed to move forward with a design. But the method you choose also must take into consideration the experience of users and stakeholders. In fact, in order to conduct socially-informed research in the design process, it is crucial to pay attention to the impacts on participants *during* the design process itself. If you do this, not only will the design be better able to meet the needs of users, but it will also tell you something about the social context of the place being designed or redesigned.

Architect Romano Nickerson, who works at a design firm specializing in medical and health care settings, described how he has witnessed the culture of a health care organization play out in the design process itself. When people who work at a clinic who are not used to having their input considered in organizational decision-making get asked to offer input on a design, their eyes light up with a bit of surprise and a glimmer of excitement. In moments when people respond like this, it becomes evident that the organization is hierarchically arranged, with a culture that allows for little input from stakeholders with different statuses. But socially-informed research requires including this input. Without knowing how an environmental services employee feels about the timing and location of hazardous waste disposal, nobody in the building can take for granted that operations run smoothly and safely. If less visible tasks (and staff) get ignored in the design process, the fallout from those ideas and people being ignored will show up in problematic places later. This is why it's crucial to include the right groups of stakeholders and the right size of groups to get all types of input, which is elaborated in Chapter 3. For now, suffice it to say that the method used in data gathering can make people feel more or less included and heard in the design process. Socially-informed research requires inclusion and plentiful opportunities for stakeholders to be heard throughout the design process, regardless of the formality and hierarchical structure of an organization.

When we match a method to a question, we need to know what each method offers us. It also helps to think about whether *quantitative or qualitative data* (or both) would be helpful. Quantitative data is made up of numbers (which can include counts of things that aren't numbers [e.g., how many lights go in a bathroom]), which means sophisticated statistical analyses can be conducted. Qualitative data is more like a set of stories or subjective experiences: patterns may be noted but more likely the main goal is depth and context rather than counting frequencies. The good news is that each of the methods described in this chapter can result in either type of data. And when we get to the data analysis discussion in Chapter 5, we'll also see ways that we can transform qualitative data into quantitative data. For now, let's sort out the benefits and drawbacks of different data-gathering methods.

In this section, I organize the methods into five primary categories: surveys; individual interviews; focus group interviews; observation; and content analysis of texts, maps, drawings, or documents. Each of these is a different approach to systematically gathering people's stories, attitudes, experiences, behaviors, and ideas. I define each of the methods and identify which types of questions they are best equipped to answer, noting the benefits and drawbacks for each. For each method, I also offer tips and a nod to the types of data analysis that the data from the method can employ (qualitative or quantitative). Table 2 notes the benefits and drawbacks of each method, for quick reference.

Throughout this section, I reference other work for any readers interested in delving into more sophisticated research methods, though my aim is to frame techniques that are accessible to beginners and can be reported to a general audience – both of which are more useful for the intended audience of this book. I also infuse elements of human-centered design into relevant sections below.

Table 2 Benefits and Drawbacks of Methods

Method	Benefits	Drawbacks
Surveys	Fast method for getting large samples and statically robust results; can add comfort because often anonymous	Harder to get depth and context to explain answers; can seem impersonal
Individual Interviews	Allows for depth and context and follow-up questions; can build trust and rapport between designer and stakeholder	Sample sizes remain small because it takes more time to collect data; harder to get at large-scale or generalizable patterns
Focus Group Interviews	Allows for depth and context and follow-up questions; faster than a series of individual interviews	Harder to capture individual stories
Observation	Can be unobtrusive and not require more time for stakeholders; can be done over time to notice change; can be done in multiple contexts and times with multiple groups	Harder to get at people's interpretation of their experience; can take more time than other methods
Content Analysis of Texts, Maps, Drawings, or Documents	Can be unobtrusive if texts are already in existence; can give context	Harder to get at people's interpretation of their experience since analysis is only of the products or texts that people have created

Surveys

I am going to go out on a limb and guess that you already know quite well what a survey is, given how ubiquitous they are in our social media feeds, at polling places, in workplace and education data collection practices, and on links printed at the bottom of store receipts to get our input on our shopping experience (and, of course, to monitor our shopping so we get advertisements that align with our buying patterns).

Architects and designers rely on survey data, as do researchers interested in large-scale patterns of human attitudes and behaviors as they may relate to the built environment. A great example of a large nationally representative study based on survey data is the 2020 "America at Home" survey (https://americaathomestudy.com/), which was meant to assess the impacts of COVID-19 on people's views about home and community design preferences. The survey data revealed, for example, that people expect several patterns to last into the future: additional garage storage, upgraded technology, using rooms for combined purposes, and using outdoor spaces to entertain family and friends.

Every time we are handed a receipt or scroll through our social media feeds, we encounter endless ways to offer our input via surveys. In my opinion, because of the proliferation of customer satisfaction surveys and an increase in the expectation that data should drive decisions in nearly every organizational and institutional realm today, surveys have become overused to the point that we survey researchers fear that nobody takes any survey very seriously anymore. Nonetheless, as with the "America at Home" survey, they remain a very efficient way to get data from and about people, and they are likely to protect people's identities since we rarely meet the person actually collecting survey data when we fill one out.

A *survey* is a set of questions, often administered anonymously, usually written down on paper or in a digital format, meant to get responses quickly from a large group of people about their attitudes, experiences, or behaviors. Questions on surveys are more often than not *closed-ended*, which means that the answer choices are provided like on a multiple-choice test. This means surveys are most useful for projects (or portions of projects) where quick and short answers without much elaboration will suffice (e.g., do you prefer the coffee maker to the right or left of the sink?). Sometimes the choices are levels of agreement or simple preferences; sometimes they are numbers attached to gradations of satisfaction or approval of some idea or thing (like the pain scale you may have seen in a medical clinic); and sometimes they are choices that are not about ranking but rather about demographics such as gender, age, geographic location, and race. Having closed-ended questions makes statistical analysis manageable, since many online survey platforms such as Qualtrics, SurveyMonkey, and Google Forms produce numeric results after your survey is completed. But surveys can include *open-ended questions* that ask respondents to type or write in a short or long text-based answer, too.

Surveys are beneficial insofar as they are relatively quick ways to get data from a large group of people. This boosts the chance of *representativeness*, which means the people in the sample closely match the traits of the population of interest (e.g., a survey of 100 high school students about their lunchroom space, where those 100 students are similar to the entire student body in that school in terms of gender, class year, race, eligibility for free or reduced lunch, and maybe even food preferences). If your sample is representative of the population, you can be more confident that the results from your research can be generalized because you have reduced the chance that certain groups' input is missing. For formal social scientific research that employs statistical analyses that include statistical significance, survey data can be particularly helpful. For socially-informed research in the design process, likely the need for this kind of robust analysis is less crucial. But ensuring that the people who take your survey represent all necessary stakeholders is key regardless of how fancy your analysis may be.

Even though surveys can help yield larger samples that better represent a population, they are limited in their capacity to allow for follow-up, clarification, or elaboration. If a person fills out a survey with their preferences for where a salad bar should go in a cafeteria, there is no opportunity to ask why they selected certain answer options (unless you include a "why" open-ended question). More importantly, if a question is unclear or could be interpreted differently by different people, there is no option to get this cleared up with the researcher. This means that the data yielded from a confusing or unclear survey question will not be useful in the end. Or, more realistically, data gathered from a survey question that has been used in dozens of previous studies may be *reliable* (meaning you'll get consistent answers each time the survey question is used), but it will not be *valid* (meaning it doesn't measure what you want it to measure).

Reliability and validity are key terms used in social science methods. You may operationalize (measure) a variable the same way over and over and get consistent results (this is reliability), but that doesn't mean the results will be helpful since you may not be operationalizing a variable accurately (this is validity). For example, you may get the same result over and over when you conduct a dozen surveys asking about color preferences with the question "Blue is really the best color, isn't it? Choose yes or no." But just because most survey data shows that people answer "no" to this (biased) question does not really tell you an accurate picture of what people's color preferences are. The question is reliable but not valid. In socially-informed research for design, it is good to use reliable measures that are valid. When no valid measures exist yet, it is better to create new measures than use old ones that don't paint an accurate picture of people's attitudes, experiences, or behaviors.

Entire books have been dedicated to effective survey design (see, e.g., Harris 2014). Survey researchers spend a lot of time thinking about best practices in the overall survey experience, including how responding to a survey can create a burden for people, as research by Rodhouse et al. (2021) details. Here I offer a few general tips for the survey design process that matter for any project, whether you're new to survey design or have been doing it for years.

How long should a survey be? The answer to this depends on the setting where people are taking the survey. If it's online and they can easily take it while they are already situated at a computer for other tasks, it could be a bit longer (maybe up to ten minutes). If it's a pen-and-paper quick response to a design exhibit where people walk by and drop their responses into an easy-to-spot box, then it should be shorter (only a few seconds).

Does the order of questions matter? Short answer: yes. Usually, it is helpful to start with questions that are easy to answer and don't call to mind anything controversial (for example, what role do you play in the organization?). For much of the research connected to design, there are probably not a lot of questions that would startle or surprise people (except maybe starting the whole thing with a blunt question about budget), and surveys used in socially-informed design are probably unlikely to be used when depth and richness are required.

One type of question used in surveys is a *matrix or composite question*. Sometimes this is referred to as a scale variable, especially if it is a series of questions that, when added together, make up a bunch of small factors that tell the story of a larger factor. For example, let's say you're interested in finding out people's preferences for traditional or modern design in home furniture. You envision that people's "scores" along this scale would range from "very traditional" to "very modern." The composite or matrix question would be made up of a series of questions in tabular form with various types of furniture in the rows, and column headings with options that range from "I really like traditional design for this furniture" to "I really like modern design for this furniture." You'd transform people's answers into numeric scores (maybe "I really like traditional design for this furniture" is a 5, and "I really like modern design for this furniture" is a 1, so more traditional taste would yield a higher score). You'd add up people's scores for each row, giving people an aggregated or scale score.

Designing the composite question should be done in such a way that people are not tempted to just *straight-line* their answers. This means we should try to prevent people from checking the same column over and over without looking at what they are answering, just to save time, thus not giving accurate responses. You can prevent this by throwing in unusual items in one of the middle rows (maybe you include a picture of a toy instead of a piece of furniture). You can also prevent this by including fewer than five or six lines in the matrix table so that there is less visual temptation to just click one column all the way down just to save time.

Another tip for survey design is to avoid *double-barreled questions*. A double-barreled question is one where you are asking about more than one variable in the same question, which means you cannot glean what people's answers mean in any sensible way. For example, if you ask the question "Do you enjoy tropical-themed decorations and open-concept living" you would not be able to tell if people's "yes" answers are about the decorations or the space; you would not know if they are answering about tropical design or wall placement. It's always better to separate out each variable so that any survey question is asking only about one at a time. This is important for interview research, too.

Survey questions are often closed-ended, with options provided where survey takers can choose one or more answers. In these cases, it is important that the possible answers are *mutually exclusive*. Answers that are mutually exclusive do not overlap in any mathematical or conceptual way. For example, when asking about income, the income ranges should not overlap (this explains why surveys include strange ranges such as $40,000–$59,999). When asking about topics that are a bit more subjective (but still asked in a closed-ended question), it is still important to provide mutually exclusive answers. This is why it is good to spend time carefully operationalizing your variables. For example, it would be problematic to ask about dining room furniture preferences with a question about the number of chairs desired and the answers choices listed as (a) at least four chairs or (b) five or more chairs. If someone wanted six chairs, both answers would work. This means they are not mutually exclusive.

The list of possible responses in closed-ended survey questions needs to be *exhaustive*. This means it is a complete list, where anyone who takes your survey can find a response choice that matches their answer. In the dining room chair example, the choices are also not exhaustive, since people who want fewer than four chairs would not see their desires reflected in the answer choices. This is not only a practical data analytical consideration; it is also an ethical one. One variable that most poignantly shows the importance of being exhaustive is race. Organizations like the US Census and the Pew Research Center are constantly working on the best ways to measure race. As flawed and limiting as any closed-ended question about identity may be, it is particularly egregious when questions about race exclude groups of people. For example, let's say you want to ask people to select their race. In your question, you only allow one answer and only include "White," "Black," and "Asian-American." In this case, you are excluding groups such as Native Americans, Pacific Islanders, Hispanic/Latina/o/x, and individuals who are multi-racial or multi-ethnic (not to mention using language across answer choices that is not parallel or consistent). One way to ensure your options constitute an exhaustive list is to include "something not listed here" or "other" (though "other" can feel a bit alienating, since it implies it is somehow not usual or normal). In this case, people can write in an option. When it comes to asking about race, another option is to ask people to check all that apply.

When creating a survey it's important to keep in mind what the eventual data analysis will look like once the data is collected. In some online survey programs such as Qualtrics, the analysis is often done for you, at least in the form of reports about answers to each individual question (this is called *univariate analysis* [one variable]). Or it allows for easy analysis of two factors together (e.g., do age groups differ in their level of preference for traditional furniture design) within the program itself (this is called *bivariate analysis*). And many programs allow you to export the data into another program that can do more sophisticated statistical analysis, such as Excel, Stata, R, SPSS, or Jamovi.

One final word about surveys that matters if you're including multiple stakeholder groups in your research. If you use any kind of survey design program that offers analytical sophistication (currently I use Qualtrics most often), you can create a survey that goes to multiple types of stakeholders, but that allows you to separate out responses by group. This can happen in a couple of different ways. First, you can create something called a *skip pattern* or *contingency question*, which is when people only get certain questions if they answer a certain way on an earlier question. In Qualtrics, this can be done using either "skip logic" or "display logic." For example, if you want to survey teachers and students about a planned high school design, you can ask the question "Are you a teacher or student?" and then create an internal feature in the survey where if they select "teacher" they are then asked questions about aligning a classroom design with pedagogical goals. If they select "student" they skip over these questions. The second way you can survey multiple groups is if you create survey questions that are asked of everyone (e.g., you could ask everyone about the alignment of classroom design and pedagogical goals, even if you don't phrase the questions using these exact words), but then when you get the results you divide the results into groups and compare how each group answered questions. In Qualtrics, this is done using the "filter" feature, where you get the results for all survey takers, but then add a filter to display results for one group at a time. These techniques allow you to collect and analyze data from multiple groups using only one survey.

Interviews

Consider these two brief interview excerpts between a designer and a client or user:

Excerpt 1:

DESIGNER: What do you want in the design for your kitchen?
CLIENT/USER: I don't know. Something old-fashioned and comfortable like I remember in my childhood home.

Excerpt 2:

DESIGNER: In the kitchen design, we can focus on style, comfort, and ways a design may connect to memories and stories that make you happy. Would you say style, comfort, or memories matter the most in how you envision the design and why?
CLIENT/USER: All three matter, but I'd say my priority is comfort because, even if a stool reminds me of my childhood kitchen, I need to make sure my furniture does not give me a backache.

In the first dialogue, the question is open-ended (i.e., answer choices are not provided) and quite general, thus allowing the interviewee to answer however they wish. In the second dialogue, the question is also open-ended, but it offers the second person some concrete (and typical) topics to focus their response. The first one allows for any factor to inform the design; the second one allows for prioritization among provided factors. Which is better? The answer depends on the goals of the project, the existing relationship between designer and client, and the familiarity of a client with elements of design.

A lot of the work designers and architects do entails having conversations with clients and other stakeholders. When a design project starts, a client interview or intake session is common. These conversations continue throughout the project to ensure that revisions and the end result meet the needs of those who will be inhabiting the design. These input moments can consist of informal conversations, after which the designer goes back to the office and uses notes and recollections from the conversation to inform the design. In this case, there are not necessarily standard questions asked; in fact, the client may initiate impromptu ideas and concerns and desires that the designer then folds into the design (or maybe rejects, depending on designer viewpoints). The gathering of ideas and desires from clients and users can also be quite formal, with a set of standard questions about specific factors – maybe even with a set of provided responses and little room for elaboration by the client or user. In this case, designers ask clients and end-users the same questions for each project, perhaps with some modules that vary depending on the type of project or client (e.g., asking questions about safety-related traffic patterns in a hospital build versus asking questions about comfort in a private living room remodel). Both of these question-and-answer tasks are types of interviews. As the examples show, though, interviews can be formal or informal, standardized or unstandardized, structured or unstructured, and everything in between. They can also vary in the ways that interviewers document the responses to their questions.

Social scientific research *interviews* are question-and-answer conversations between interviewers and interviewees aimed at systematically eliciting and noticing patterns across interviewee responses that go beyond noting the individual needs of those people who are interviewed. Being systematic is important regardless of whether the interview questions are exactly the same each time interviews are conducted, whether they are offered in a formal or informal setting or documenting, or whether they consist of open- or closed-ended questions. It is also important regardless of whether the interviews happen with a large group of people involved in one design project or a few people at a time involved in many projects over time. All of these "either/or" decisions are detailed below.

Often interviews are either recorded (with permission) and transcribed, or they include a lot of note-taking by the interviewer or a research collaborator or assistant. In either case, the interviewer needs to focus on the conversation at hand and take steps to prevent errors that are common when we try to rely only on memory. If we rely on our memory of conversations, it is hard to be sure that we are getting a client's story right, and it is really difficult to trust that we are noticing patterns in their needs and desires. This focus and diligence are part of a systematic approach to interview design.

Everyday conversations and research interviews operate differently. In everyday conversations, I strive to listen and recall what my friends and colleagues say. I don't take notes, and if I get a piece of information wrong I can check back with them. My goal is to be a good friend or colleague, not to analyze what they're saying in any systematic way. When I conduct interviews, I operate a bit differently. Specifically, I ask questions in order to get particular answers that can help me make decisions informed by patterns I see in interviewee responses. If I'm wearing a researcher hat, I'm more of an investigative journalist – but one who is interested in data patterns in addition to the compelling story.

Doing interviews already feels a bit more artificial than an impromptu conversation; interviewers have to think about what kind of stage to set for conducting the interviews. While Chapter 4 details the importance of place, and while each designer operates a bit differently, more often than not designers will go to the location that is convenient for a client to gather their input. In projects at my college with which I've been involved, for example, the architects and designers made the trip to Walla Walla to get feedback about their designs. But a handful of people here also made a couple of trips to see other designs in person. At no point did I go to the architecture firm's building itself.

When conducting interviews, you have to make some decisions about how formal they feel. Formality can include questions of dress and use of bodies (casual or professional, sitting or walking around), location (neutral coffee shop, designer- or client-hosted), and even voice and affect (personalized or professional). These decisions should be based on the goals of your project and your own preferred method of connecting with clients and users. They also require analyzing the benefits and drawbacks of using standardized or non-standardized questions, incorporating open- or closed-ended questions (which leads to qualitative or quantitative data), and various ways to document interviewee responses. I'll talk about each of these topics in turn.

How standardized should interview questions be? The answer to this depends on how precise you want to be when it comes to noticing patterns across clients/users. Think about this: if you ask everyone in an interview project exactly the same questions in the same order, it would be easy to compare their answers with confidence that these answers did not depend on how you worded a question as you went from person to person. In other words, if you ask people differently worded questions, that wording can affect their answers. So, if your goal is precision and capacity to make confident claims about the patterns in the data across all participants, then standardizing the questions is a good idea.

But what if standardizing the questions feels too stiff or unnatural? What if your inclination is to create a rapport with interviewees that includes allowing them to go on tangents in their answers, tailoring questions to their particular situation, and making sure you have a lot of detail and context surrounding their answers? In that case, non-standardized interviews are better. While you would have a harder time making claims about patterns across interviewees, you'd meet their individual needs a bit better. Further, unless you can memorize a standardized interview script well enough to make it seem unrehearsed and conversational, a non-standardized interview would feel a bit more like a natural conversation.

A nice middle ground is semi-standardized interviews, which is asking interviewees mostly the same questions in mostly the same order, and with mostly the same wording. Interviews are always a bit of a performance, but tailoring them at least somewhat can make them feel more natural and less rehearsed. Because interviewing people usually involves tangents and multiple interpretations, formulating questions that allow for storytelling or clarification can be helpful and feel more natural. But if you enter an interview with no set of topics or questions (even loosely worded), then it would be hard to know if your designs over time or across constituencies are meeting people's needs. For example, you may want to ask people in a work building about the bathrooms you design. You want to find out about cleanliness: how people define it, how surfaces get cleaned, and how clean people desire the space to be. For any of these topics, you'd tailor the wording of questions to the role of the person being interviewed, and to the type of bathroom being designed. In this case, "what constitutes a clean bathroom" could be a prompt in a semi-standardized set of interview topics, where the question could be asked in different ways. More importantly, and likely based on experience with different clients, users, surfaces, and designs, you would have *prompts* in the interview question document, which are notes to yourself to be sure and follow up with certain questions depending on their answers. For example, you could have a follow-up prompt about actual cleaning products used if you were interviewing environmental services or custodial staff, and about the perception of cleanliness to others who use the bathroom. In either case, the topic is the same and the question may even be worded similarly, but the exact wording and follow-up questions would vary from person to person. This way, you'd have enough standardization to make claims about overall client/user views on cleanliness at the same time you'd allow varied stakeholder needs to be discussed. For the immediate design, you'd thus have interview findings that represent shared views and experiences as well as individualized ones. If you keep track of the impact of your design across time and/or projects, some semblance of standardization can make noticing patterns or trends of your entire design dossier easier to spot.

Open- and closed-ended questions matter when we think about whether our research is quantitative or qualitative. Both can be done in interview research. In socially-informed design, designers need to have an idea of the types of answers from clients and users that will help them move thoughtfully (and quickly) to design decisions. It is also important to think about how the questions asked need to ensure that people feel as if their voices matter in the entire process. Often people think that this means you have to use very open-ended questions, so that any kind of response is allowed. This feels more freeing for interviewees, as if they are not being put into preconceived boxes. But it is also possible to ask questions where you provide answers that are based on solid past research or experience and that may allow an interviewee to focus their thoughts on a smaller number of options. Have you heard about the psychological research where offering too many choices can actually stunt people from making a choice at all (DeAngelis 2004)? Sometimes if we are given a few options that, when we think about it, actually capture things that matter to us, we can feel like our responses matter a lot. As an exercise, when people ask "how are you?" this is tremendously open-ended. We can answer any way we choose. But if someone who has paid attention to the kinds of things that matter to a lot of people when they think about their well-being asks, "would you say you are feeling more or less tired than yesterday?" we can also feel heard. Sometimes having a finite set of choices that capture what is important to the situation at hand can yield more honest and accurate responses, which can lead to better outcomes that are based on those responses. When you think about what to ask people, then, don't assume that open-ended questions will always get more accurate responses, and be sure that closed-ended questions include well-informed and complete sets of response options. Just like with survey questions, where you need to make sure your list of possible options is exhaustive, people who are interviewed using closed-ended questions should feel as if their answers can be found from among the ones offered.

Do standardization of interviews and open-endedness of questions relate to each other? They can, but not necessarily. You could have standardized interviews made up entirely of open-ended questions, and unstandardized interviews made up of closed-ended questions. So, when you think about how formal you want the interviews to be, pay attention to whether you want to prioritize the ability to systematically note patterns across interviewees and not let question wording influence their answers. This is about standardization. Also, pay attention to how much you want people to focus their answers on specific topics rather than broad ones. This is about closed- or open-ended questions.

One last element of formality deals with the choreography of the interview itself, although this topic also relates to how the interview responses will be used more generally. How do you envision being able to remember what people's answers are when you interview them? Should you place a recording device on the table (or hit record in a video chat)? Should you take notes or just focus on maintaining eye contact with people being interviewed? What does that "dance" look like, both in terms of your usual presence in professional interactions and in terms of your goals for the interview itself? While analyzing data gathered using interviews (and other methods) is the subject of Chapter 5, it is important to think about what you want the data to look like as you design the data-gathering tool. This means you should think about whether you'll record audio and video of an interview, simply take notes, both, or neither before you do any interviews. If you want direct quotes, recordings help (though transcribing interviews word for word takes a long time). If you want quick answers where a checklist that you hold onto fits well into the setting, then you may not need a recording. For most interactions between designers and users/clients, a recording is probably not needed. But taking detailed notes is often helpful. This is why having two people present during any interview is a great idea: one to ask the questions and maintain eye contact and keep the conversation moving fluidly and naturally, and the other to take notes so that people do not need to rely on memory to inform the design. And importantly, if any recordings take place, people being recorded must agree to this before you hit the "record" button.

The aforementioned definition of interviews includes the phrase "systematically eliciting and noticing patterns across interviewee responses." Importantly, "across" can occur by gathering input from many stakeholders for one project, or it can occur over a long period of time in multiple projects with one client or user at a time. Even in one project, there are multiple points in time when interviews may be useful. After all, the central premise of socially-informed design is to thoughtfully and systematically gather input before the design, as the design is created and revised, after the design is implemented to see how it is being used, and later as future designs are informed by past input.

Focus Groups

The previous section detailed interviews as a useful technique for gathering client and user ideas and desires, including questions surrounding how standardized, open-ended, and formally-documented they should be. These can happen in one-on-one conversations to be sure. But often in design professions, especially in large-scale projects where input is gathered from a wide variety of constituencies in a short amount of time, interviews occur with groups. These are called *focus group interviews* – question-and-answer conversations between interviewers and a group of interviewees aimed at systematically eliciting and noticing patterns across interviewee responses and noting group-specific needs of those people who are interviewed. Like one-on-one interviews, focus groups can occur at multiple stages of the design process. The main difference is that the input is gathered from a group of people responding at the same time in the same (digital or physical) place.

Focus groups are a common method in market research dedicated to determining how people view a certain product or process. Whether movie producers are trying to decide which ending of a movie would better resonate with an audience, or a soap company is trying to decide which scent makes people feel cleaner, focus groups are useful for getting rich and contextualized data quickly.

Focus groups are also common in human-centered design (and UX) research. Sometimes they are called focus sessions, they occur multiple times during the design process, and they often involve interview questions alongside other methods such as sticker voting, card sorting, gallery walks, or storyboarding (some of which are discussed below in the "Observation" section). In this kind of research, *affinity maps* are also sometimes used to see how people's reactions to ideas may cluster together into themes. These can be used in group sessions with people where they put ideas about their responses to your questions onto sticky notes, and these are organized into groups that seem similar. How they're grouped depends on what your question is and whether you are seeking to find common or uncommon answers to your questions.

Usually focus groups are made up of five to eight people who gather in one physical (or virtual) space to talk about their views about a certain topic, experience, or product. The point of the data-gathering is not just to get individual-level input; the conversation itself can shed light on people's ideas. Benefits of this kind of group interview include gathering data quickly, as well as capturing how people's views actually work in real time (since we're often influenced by others through conversations we have with them). But the realness of the conversation can also be a drawback, especially if people who are unlikely to speak up in a room where other voices dominate end up having their views excluded. If any of us has an opinion that we fear may be unpopular, it is all the more difficult to express it if we're in a large group as opposed to a one-on-one conversation with someone. This is why it's important to include a skilled facilitator of group conversations, whether it's you or a colleague. Just as with individual interviews, having two people involved can help: one who can facilitate the conversation (including maintaining eye contact, keeping track of tangents, and facilitating conversation such that quieter participants are asked to share ideas), and one who can take notes.

Whether a focus group is recorded or not depends on the same questions mentioned in the previous discussion about interviews.

Because they're efficient and mimic real decision-making conversations in various settings, focus groups are ideal if the design project involves lots of people across different stakeholder groups. Sometimes it's useful to have multiple focus groups, which could be defined in terms of commonalities or differences among stakeholders. Designing focus group interview questions (as with survey and interview questions) can either be done such that everyone gets the same question or such that different groups get different questions (or prompts in an interview). If a focus group is made up of different stakeholder types, then the wording of questions needs to allow for everyone to answer regardless of their role. If focus groups are divided by stakeholder type, then it is easier to ask questions tailored to each specific focus group.

Observation

Sometimes I joke with students that sociologists are just a bunch of creepy voyeurs secretly watching people in public places and making claims based on patterns they witness. While it is technically allowed to observe public behavior without people's consent in the American Sociological Association Code of Ethics, I want to emphasize that this depiction of sociological researchers is a caricature. Certainly observation of human behavior (even without talking with people being observed) can bring to mind images of mad social scientists in lab coats, but it is true that we can learn a lot from watching what people do. Since conducting large-scale experiments of big groups of people is both cumbersome and often unethical, observational research in sociology (and related fields such as anthropology) is one of the best techniques sociologists can do to understand how people behave in their "natural environments." Even if the environment is artificial, as a full-size mock-up of a hospital wing made out of cardboard is, people's actions may speak louder than words. This is where on-site ethnographic research and simulation observation in the form of gallery walks and exhibits come into play.

Ethnographic research is defined as deep, frequent, and systematic observation of people's behaviors and experiences at a site of interest. It is often paired with interviews of those people, to make sure any claims made by observers accurately depict people's motivations, thoughts, and opinions. Many ethnographic research projects also include maps or drawings of spaces, people's movements and roles within the spaces, and notes about how time or group composition may change the way a space is used. Sometimes I have heard designers and architects describe one version of this kind of data gathering as "neighborhood walks." A primary goal of this kind of research is to gain as much depth and context about the people and place being observed. Generalizability to a larger population or different place matters less than getting at detailed and thorough explanation of what's going on in that locale with that specific group of people.

For design research, ethnography can be helpful if a space will be occupied by different people across time (maybe even seasonally), or if the social situation of the people who'll use the space changes over time. It can also be a useful method in spaces where the feelings and values of people involved may be hard to see or hard to ask about. For example, redesigning a sleeping space in a shelter for women and children who have experienced or survived domestic abuse should include not just surface-level data that could be gleaned from a quick survey or short interviews of staff members. Watching how people engage with the current space, spending time gaining the trust of residents, and asking open-ended questions that allow for interpretation and storytelling are necessary.

Another type of ethnographic observation can include setting up a simulated design (perhaps even actual size), and then observing how people use the space. While this does not necessarily require a longitudinal (over a long period of time) design, it is important to observe people's interactions with the design at more than one point in time, and perhaps with different combinations of people who will eventually occupy that designed space. These kinds of methods yield similar social moments as an art gallery or exhibit – people seeing different content visually represented, responding to it, and meandering from item to item to digest the content and share ideas.

Gallery walks and exhibits are two of these types of simulation design methods, which allow for designers to observe and notice patterns in people's responses as they examine design mock-ups, color palettes, or images of design elements. *Gallery walks* are defined as organized meanderings of a group of people who are asked to respond to some kind of displayed content, often done in round robin or station-to-station fashion. I used this method in teaching fairly often, when the content could be a summary of a text, a research design, or even a diagram or chart interpreting data. People who are responding to others' content offer feedback in various forms such as informal discussion, brief ideas shared on sticky notes, brainstorming, *card sorting activities* (a UX method where participants are given cards that are either blank with a call for them to note salient words or observations from a given set of ideas, or that include salient choices on them that they then sort, prioritize, or cluster with others), or Q&A sessions. *Exhibits* – especially ones in architecture and design fields – consist of showcasing a design in some kind of visual format (drawings, animations, slides, 3-D renderings, full-size mock-ups), and then asking people to respond to the design.

Gallery walks and exhibits are opportunities for gathering input via interviews or surveys as well, since asking people questions about which visual elements they prefer maps easily onto interview and survey question sets. Asking people questions about what they see is a common technique in design research. But these kinds of observation methods also include moments when designers can observe people's behaviors in the gallery walk or exhibit itself: what facial expressions are they using? What does their body language say about their attraction or revulsion to a design? What are they saying to others as they meander through the visual representations of the design? What seems to confuse people? Here, the formal gathering of data from people about what they think of the design is easy to manage via individual or group interviews or a quick survey. But there are informal cues that can be part of the design research: how people talk about what their thoughts are about the design can be fruitful fodder for input, too.

Sometimes in sociological (and UX) research participants are the ones collecting their own data, either via photos or videos, or by journaling in writing or drawing maps of their experiences. Often these tasks are accompanied by a request for users to note how they're feeling or why they've chosen to document their experience in a certain way. These observations, made by the users themselves, can then be gathered and reviewed by a researcher to see if there are any similarities or differences among people who participated.

Content Analysis of "Texts"

A fruitful location for design research is not only found by asking people questions or observing their behaviors. The "texts" that people produce – writings, images, documents, artifacts, drawings – can also constitute the data that designers use in their socially-informed research. This is called *content analysis*. Some of these texts are produced via other data-gathering techniques, such as drawings that can be analyzed to look for common themes, or diaries that users write about their use of a space at different times of day or days of the week. Designers who collect data through sticky note ideas, maps, and even ethnographic observations (in the form of field notes) can analyze those documents for common themes, too. In all of these cases, the data that is analyzed comes from people; it's just that the data is not necessarily collected by asking people direct questions via surveys or interviews.

Content analyzed by designers throughout the research can also include documents produced by the people who are either funding or eventually inhabiting the design. These documents can include maps, websites, organization by-laws, existing images or objects that symbolize the organization, and even informal notes that may be visible in places such as break rooms, individual work spaces, closets, or bulletin boards. Why might these objects, documents, and images be worthy of study? Because they can shed light on the values, beliefs, and practices of a group of people who use that space. This is why looking at both formal and informal texts and artifacts is helpful. If designers and architects want to understand what is important to people who will use the space, it is a great idea to study the objects, images, and words they use in their everyday lives.

The culture of a place is often uncovered not just by asking people questions or watching their behaviors, but by noticing what they display to (or maybe even hide from) others in their current spaces. Being intentional and systematic about including the materials and words used by people for whom you are designing a space is crucial. This can take the form of note-taking during ethnographic observation or including additional elements in mapping or measuring sessions (e.g., look at the types of personalized objects people display in their work spaces – does the display include family photos? Plants? Do different spaces or do different people display different amounts or types of personalization? Why?). Material, visual, and textual displays on websites or other public-facing materials can tell a story of what an organization values (e.g., do they feature mostly people or technology? Do they share stories or numeric data? Do they focus on images or text? What are the central messages of these images and texts?). While talking with people who do or will occupy a design is key to knowing whether the design is being socially-informed, don't forget to take a systematic approach to observing their display of values, beliefs, and everyday practices through objects and words. These, like survey responses, are also data that can be analyzed to inform a design.

How Do You Use More Than One Method at a Time? Understanding Triangulation

When we try to answer a question, it is helpful to come at it from different angles, or to gather information from more than one source. Collecting data in socially-informed research works the same way: sometimes finding out how well a design is working requires asking about it using multiple methods. This is called *triangulation*: using more than one research method to answer a question. Some examples of this include the following:

- Asking focus group participants to draw maps and share ideas about the best way to design a hallway
- Interviewing a few key stakeholders and then following up with a large group via surveys
- Conducting an exhibition with a short paper survey for feedback
- Offering a 30-second digital survey where the answers are used in follow-up interview questions
- Holding a focus group session in the middle of a simulated space to get feedback

Triangulation can be helpful when we are not sure if the one method we use to collect data is the best method, or when we sense that we are missing some crucial voices who got missed because they could not access one method (e.g., schedule conflicts that make attending a focus group difficult, but that make taking a survey possible). Triangulation can bolster our confidence that we have found helpful patterns and trends in one data-gathering method because the patterns appear in another data-gathering method. Further, they can help us see when our results from one method fail to capture the full picture of people's experiences with the design. Essentially, the more angles we use to come at a problem, the more creative we can be and the more sure we can be that our design or solution is a well-informed and inclusive one. A mixed methods approach can bolster this assurance.

Chapter 4 delves into how time works in a socially-informed research process, but here it is helpful to note that one way to triangulate is to use different methods at different times during the design process. For example, you may start with focus groups, and then use a simulation or exhibit after a mock-up is made. While it is not easy to find precise patterns that may change over time while using different methods at different time periods in the design process (because the change in patterns may be due to the method itself), it is possible to match methods to steps in the research process, thus yielding better-informed design. Case in point: you can't do a simulation using a mock-up until you make one and you likely would not make a mock-up of a space without first talking with stakeholders via surveys, interviews, or focus groups.

Earlier I shared a story about architect Romano Nickerson's work in health care settings. In a related story, he shared that a full-size mock-up of a hospital wing was created after some conversations with health care professionals. When parents and potential patients walked through the simulated space and shared their views (as in focus group research), one mother noticed that there was no space in the patient bathroom to change a diaper for a child older than toddler age. This was a problem, she asserted, because her child was twelve years old and had this need. In this case, if the design process had only included one step in the data-gathering process and had only used one method (and one stakeholder group), the design would not have met the needs of all patients, nor would it have been a good example of universal design (meeting everyone's needs by virtue of meeting needs of those who have unique access or ability issues).

How Do You Pay Attention to Aesthetics and Accessibility? Audio, Tactile, and Visual Elements of Data Collection

The method you use to collect data is important, but equally important is what the data collection sounds, looks, and feels like. We use our senses in any research method, and being systematic with how we pay attention to our senses is helpful in data gathering. Designers and architects already know this – how a space looks, feels, sounds, and even smells can affect users' desire to be in that space, and can affect the likelihood of activities that are meant to take place in that space. For example, if the lighting is too dim, it can be hard to see tasks. Loud noises can interrupt workflow. Scratchy fabric can dissuade people from sitting in a chair. And we all know that good ventilation is important for bathrooms!

In the data collection phase of research, paying attention to these things matters, too. Here it is important to think about which method may best capture the sensory information that will be most useful in a design. If the key desire of users is physical comfort, then including feedback on tactile elements of the design through interviews or sticker voting may be helpful. If a goal is creating the most effortless traffic flow for people moving through a space, then using video or visual observation techniques (including mapping) of people's movements will be best. If movement of objects in a space is important or if assessing whether wall and door placement works, then creating full-size mock-ups of objects, walls, and doorways is a great idea. While decibel measurement devices are useful for checking auditory problems in a space, it can also be useful to use audio recording to talk with people about the space. Listening to what's going on in a space is great, but giving people a chance to share ideas with someone whose main job is to listen can be helped with digital recordings.

A good test in the research process is to ask what senses will be invoked by users who occupy the space. What I'm suggesting here is to take a step back and also ask what senses should be involved in the process of seeking user input in the first place. Test the smells, sights, sounds, and tactile sensations as you get feedback in a systematic way. Not only does this capture the important elements of the future design, but it also humanizes the design research process. After all, we are all sensory beings. Architects and designers will make better designs if people have a chance to engage their senses as they navigate a new design and imagine how it may work for their lives. This is especially important for people who have disabilities that make accessing the sensory elements of a design challenging. Problems can be found in designs that don't allow adequate space for movement for differently abled bodies, or poor lighting for those with visual impairments. But problems can also appear in designs (and data collection efforts about the designs) that fail to recognize the importance of visibility challenges, smell sensitivities, auditory signals, or tactile sensitivities to people who will eventually inhabit a design. Figuring out how sensory differences impact people's experiences with a design should be part of the data-gathering process in design research. This is a key element of universal design, because it helps everyone feel as if they belong in any space.

How Should Thinking about Analysis Inform the Choice of Method? Thinking Ahead to the Future "How"

Earlier in this chapter, I discussed the importance of creating survey questions that include answers that are both mutually exclusive (no overlaps) and exhaustive (a full list of possible answers). I also discussed in chapter 1 how knowing what kind of question you're asking will point you to gathering certain kinds of data – perhaps qualitative or quantitative. Paying attention to these kinds of things in the design of the data-gathering tool will help with data analysis later on. While sometimes our questions change once we dive into data collection, we still need to be thoughtful about how useful our dataset will be as we frame our questions and design our data collection tools.

As a research project is itself designed, it is also important to decide how much data is enough to move forward and to decide whose data counts the most along the way. Realistically, it's also about funding. And it's about the experience level of the design team. If you have hundreds of hours of design experience with projects like these, that matters. But remember, as noted earlier, sometimes the data that can be most helpful is the singular voice of a stakeholder pointing out something that did not occur to anyone else in the room. This is a burden for those individual voices, so it's important for designers to not use only their past experience to inform design. New ideas can come from patterns in the data that demonstrate collective sentiments from stakeholders, and they can come from singular participants whose needs and wants may be less visible to others entrenched in habitual experiences in the place and in the design profession. Designing a data-gathering process that results in answers to your research question is key, but so is allowing some flexibility in that process so that new ideas can be shared.

References

DeAngelis, Tori. 2004. "Too Many Choices?" *Monitor on Psychology* 35(6): 56.

Harris, David F. 2014. *The Complete Guide to Writing Questionnaires*. Durham, NC: I&M Press.

Rodhouse, Joseph, Tyler Wilson, and Heather Ridolfo. 2021. "Questionnaire Complexity, Rest Period, and Response Likelihood in Establishment Surveys." *Journal of Survey Statistics and Methodology* 00: 1–19.

Choosing a Sample and Communicating with People during the Research Process – The WHO

3

Recently I had a conversation with market research expert Jaimie Thimmesh Rachie. I asked her if she ever participated in a project where the bottom line was not necessarily about profit, but rather about meeting the needs of a population that an organization was having a hard time reaching. She told me the story of a former client, a non-profit Buddhist center whose leaders wanted to do a better job of engaging young adults in their work. They had a good grasp of how to meet the needs of older and more established clientele, but their existing attempts at engaging youth were met with radio silence. They wanted young people to trust them and become more involved. To research possible strategies, Jaimie's firm looked into what the existing attempts to reach a wide audience looked like.

Through user interviews, they discovered not only that young people were unsure what the mission of the organization was (even wondering if it was a cult), but they also thought the website was not very user-friendly. In contrast, older individuals saw the website as useful and interesting. The market research team realized that it was not possible to have one website cater to both audiences, so they designed a second website specifically targeted at youth. This second site featured community stories and more updated navigation.

Jaimie likened the example to the magazines *Vogue* and *Teen Vogue* – both under the same organizational umbrella but divided into versions that meet different needs of different audiences. The market research team would not have figured this out without recognizing the need to separate the organization's audience into subgroups. The research team's job was not only to recognize the goals of the organization but also to step back and know what

DOI: 10.4324/9781003183228-4

questions to ask, what data to gather, and – as highlighted in this chapter – whose voices to include in the research. Regardless of whether a design is of a website or a building, the people who are included in the design process must be thoughtfully considered in socially-informed research.

Who Are You as an Architect or Designer? Understanding the Designer Role and Empathizing with People Who Participate in Research

What do you do when your vision contradicts the wishes of users for a space you design? What if you're right and they're wrong, or vice versa – and how do you know whose vision to follow? How does being embedded or distanced from a group of people who are participating in your research matter? In the Introduction, I talked about the importance of balancing the needs of users and clients along with your vision as a designer or architect. Here I elaborate on this balance, with a focus on ethics, expertise, etic/emic approaches, and empathy. Because socially-informed research has human relationships at the heart of the process, it's crucial to talk about the roles and relationships of the humans involved.

Socially-informed research requires maintaining a high standard of research ethics, a term introduced in Chapter 1. In sociology, we aim to do no harm, to protect participant privacy (especially if their views may somehow have negative consequences such as embarrassment or a harmed reputation), and to ensure that researcher bias doesn't stand in the way of participant voices. While socially-informed research used in the design process may not require submitting a formal research protocol to a human subjects review committee (unless the designer plans to use the data to write a formal academic paper), ethics are still important to ensure. It's just that the consideration of ethics may occur in more informal ways. Even so, designers who gather input from people to inform the design should create processes that ensure ethical collection and use of data, and document research steps where this takes place.

Do you find yourself attaching your name only to design projects where you control every design decision? Does it make you nervous to work on a design that allows for style and aesthetic input of others who are not designers themselves? If you find yourself answering yes to either of these questions, then participating in socially-informed research in the design process may seem challenging at first. This is not to say that having an opinion about what constitutes good design is by itself a problem, or necessarily unethical. Rather, one of the most important ethical elements to attend to in research is *bias* – subjective opinions that may sway the outcomes of research. While being subjective and having opinions about what to do in a design are totally appropriate, it's important to set aside personal views in the midst of gathering input from others even if they're informed by rigorous and sound expertise. It's impossible to be totally objective, since our values shape everything from aesthetic preference to social views that inform a design. But sometimes what we want or think can get in the way of allowing others' voices to be part of the design process. In socially-informed research, we need to pay attention to the role of bias – our own and that of others. Later in this chapter, I discuss how to make sure your research process is transparent to those who are invited to participate so that they know how their input will be used to inform the design. Part of that transparency is ensuring that participants know how you see your role in the process. In socially-informed research, the people who gather data should spend time considering two things that relate to the designer role: positionality and reflexivity.

Positionality refers to the ways that the social position of a researcher relates to the people involved in the research (or the community context in which the research is taking place). We all occupy various social positions, sometimes several at the same time. I am a middle-aged white woman who lives in the US and who speaks English fluently. I also am highly educated and have an occupation that has a lot of prestige. This means that my social position may influence whether somebody I just meet (who knows these things about me) feels comfortable talking with me. Someone may feel intimidated or not, depending on their social position. In most discussions among social scientists, positionality is important because if someone is intimidated by someone who is conducting research, they may feel a bit less likely to trust them or offer honest input, especially about personal opinions that they hope are not connected with their names. Some of this depends on whether a participant trusts authority figures or formal institutions. Or, if a researcher occupies a social position that a client or user feels is beneath them, then the researcher's voice or views may be taken less seriously. In most instances, positionality matters because we respond to people we don't know very well based on our perception of their social statuses. Sometimes we get it wrong, sometimes we judge or exclude people (even unintentionally), and sometimes we mistrust people who seem different from us. It is helpful for researchers to be aware of this as they offer their words as a design authority, and as they listen to others' words whose ideas may be taken more or less seriously depending on how biased they may be about the researcher's social status. For any researcher, approaching the design and data-gathering with humility and openness is a crucial part of socially-informed research.

Reflexivity is when a researcher is aware of the way that their presence in the research process may shape how participants respond, and then adjust the research approach to lessen bias. It requires anyone on the research team (designers, builders, architects, contractors, government officials, and others) to examine their own values and beliefs, set them aside as they interpret input from others, and use that input without judgment. While the presence of any researcher will impact the outcome of a study, and while it is impossible to remove all bias from social situations (including gathering input from users), it is important to make efforts to reduce that impact. This can occur in a few different ways. First, even if you start with a desired outcome or hypothesis, you should be prepared to have the results from others' input challenge that outcome or guess. In other words, you should be prepared to be wrong. Second, you should spend more time listening than talking. This is good advice even if your data collection process is a written survey or observation. When I say "talking," I include thinking and discussing the ideas only with others on the design team. Input from clients, funders, and users can only be taken seriously if those gathering the input listen and let the design be informed by others' words. This is tricky since sometimes others' ideas can be really strange. To be ethical in socially-informed research is to consider your reflexive role, even as you maintain the value of your own design expertise.

A designer's *expertise* – their own credentials, approaches, and knowledge – must be present in any socially-informed research. There's a reason you've spent so much time working on your practice and gaining and applying your design knowledge. You know design! And even though the input from users, funders, and clients shapes design outcomes, you can incorporate these ideas without sacrificing your own goals as a designer. This is a tricky balance.

I hope that, after you read this book, you can trust your expertise not just as a designer, but also as a researcher. Part of the trust of clients and users should come in the form of them believing that you're qualified (without being intimidating), that you have a design vision, and that you have design credentials. But another large part of that trust comes when you demonstrate that your input process is socially-informed. If people who are invited to offer their ideas about a design know what, why, and how you're using those ideas to inform the design, and that you're being systematic, thoughtful, and ethical about it, then your expertise as a researcher is also informing their trust.

Expertise matters at all career stages. I had a chance to talk with McKenna Vetter, who had just started a position as an architect after graduating from college the year before. McKenna became interested in architecture as a child when she would accompany her dad to his construction sites; she was intrigued with watching how a building could go from the idea stage to physical completion and saw herself being able to continue this childhood excitement in a career in architecture. When I talked with her, she had been working at an architecture and design firm in Las Vegas for nine months and expressed excitement for some of the cool hotel projects she and her colleagues were working on. She talked about her thesis project from last year, where she had proposed interviewing parents, children, and medical professionals about a pediatric hospital design. While her current position is more behind-the-scenes in production, she is eager to talk with clients and users to put into play what she had worked on in school. She is paying attention to how her more senior colleagues talk with clients and she is connecting with other women in the field who find that gaining status and expressing their design voice can be a challenge in a male-dominated profession. In our conversation, my favorite moment was when she said that in Las Vegas she and her colleagues hear about plenty of nutty ideas from clients. I tell this story because McKenna is someone who has a good design sense and confidence to know what client ideas may be important to revise (or even ignore), but who has not yet had a chance to be on the front lines of data collection and analysis from people who will engage with her designs. Socially-informed design does not mean sacrificing your own design vision, even if it's a vision that is in its beginning stages. If everything was built based on client and user ideas, well, buildings would fall apart, and the "mind's eye" vision of what a design would look like if actually built would not be informed by proper design expertise. It is also important to recognize that career stage may matter, where architects and designers who have not yet had a chance to build a massive portfolio or gain much experience collecting data from users probably feel less confident in their designs than more senior colleagues. And senior designers and architects may find it useful to mentor newer members of a team about how to balance expertise and empathy for users (without getting overconfident, since it's never too late to learn new ideas even from people outside of our professional realm). In other words, design expertise is required for any project (hence the years of training, theses, and practice), but it should not come at the expense of empathy for those who will eventually engage with the design. An architect or interior designer at any career stage can hone research expertise as they continue to grow in design expertise.

How close or distant a researcher is from the group of people, culture, or geographic location of a design project matters. The question of social distance calls to mind the terms etic and emic. *Etic research* is when a researcher remains outside the group, activity, or culture being examined, whereas *emic research* requires the researcher to be embedded within that group, activity, or culture (Lucas 2016). As Chapter 2 detailed, different methods bring a researcher closer to people who are engaged with the research. Surveys are a bit distant since they can be administered without being physically present, and can be conducted by people whom participants never meet. But ethnographic observation and one-on-one interviews require at least some embedding or presence in the setting where observations take place. Sometimes etic/emic are referenced in terms of objectivity and subjectivity, where etic appears to be more objective because the researcher remains an outside (and presumably objective) observer. But, since researchers always bring values to the table, etic and emic are more useful to name the consideration of what will be most useful for a project. Sometimes it is best to remain outside to make observations, and sometimes it helps to get to better data by being embedded (and thus more susceptible to subjective experience). Thus, surveys are more etic, and interviews and ethnographic observation are more emic. While either can work, as you design your research it is important to inform your research with thoughtful consideration of when it is more helpful for you to be an outsider (etic) or an insider (emic).

Empathy is the ability to see yourself in someone else's shoes and to understand what others are experiencing. This differs from sympathy, where we may feel for a person in another set of circumstances but we really have no chance of being in that precise circumstance. For example, I can sympathize with cat owners about the need to have part of a room for a litter box, I will never get a cat (I'm allergic) and so I cannot fully empathize. For socially-informed research in the design process, it is important for designers to be as empathetic as possible, even if they have not or cannot experience the exact same thing as users. This is a central tenet of human-centered design, where the end product needs to take into consideration the needs and desires of those who will engage with it. If these needs and desires are not considered, the design won't work. To wrap empathy into research during the design process is to embed moments when people's true feelings and experiences can be gathered, observed, and used to make a design better. Designers – while they may not know what it's like to be a restaurant server, parent of an ill child, or apartment dweller – should spend a considerable amount of time thinking and building thorough and thoughtful data-gathering processes that ensure people's honest ideas are shared. While a designer cannot truly walk in someone else's shoes, they can create simulations or mock-ups, survey questions, and observational techniques (and triangulation thereof) that come close. So, if I was designing a bedroom where the cat needed plenty of space and furnishings, I'd work with a client by asking good questions, showing multiple visual and mock-up designs, and maybe even spending some time getting to know the cat (from a distance).

Ethics, expertise, etic/emic approaches, and empathy all matter for socially-informed research in design, and they all inform each other. Maintaining high standards to ensure safety and comfortability for people who participate in your research (ethics) should coincide with a balance between trustworthy authority (expertise), understanding of insider or outsider status of a designer (emic/etic), and plenty of space and time for people to walk you through their experiences even if you haven't actually walked a mile in their shoes (empathy). After all, people are more likely to give you honest feedback if they trust you, if they feel like their input matters and won't be used against them, and if they feel like you "get them." This is a good set of elements to include in any research and design process, just as it is in any relationship that we have with other people.

Whose Data Should You Gather? Choosing a Sample Size and Deciding Types of Constituents

In Chapter 1, I discussed the importance of carefully crafting a good research question and selecting variables to include in the research. Chapter 2 covered various methods used to gather data. This chapter delves more deeply into the people part of the research project. In the rest of this chapter, I discuss the selection and roles of people who participate in the research (the sample), strategies for communication among people involved, and ways that social inequalities and power may matter in all of this.

Imagine being approached to design a playground in a local neighborhood, and you want to find out what local residents may want in the playground design. For this kind of design, there are several constituencies that matter beyond the design team: neighbors, city officials, parents and caregivers, and, of course, children. You probably would not need to include every single person in all of these categories in order to feel like you're informed about various constituency views. But you'd carefully ensure that all constituencies are represented and that all who represent any constituency are able to provide input that captures the views of others in that group. You would also want to set up an ethical and empathetic data collection process where people felt that their voices mattered.

Who are we really talking about when we are talking about groups of people involved in the design process? Throughout this book I use the terms constituent, stakeholder, user, and client to refer to the people whose ideas are gathered and to capture the varied types of vocabulary used in design projects when referring to the people involved. But each of these terms means something slightly different. User and client are easiest to distinguish. Users (sometimes referred to as end-users) are people who actually inhabit or use the designed spaces, such as patients and medical professionals in a clinic or residents in a home. Clients are people who are initiating and likely funding the project. In the case of private dwelling designs and remodels, clients and users may be the same people (in which case I may use these terms interchangeably). In the case of larger projects the client may be a tiny portion of the user group (e.g., the leaders of a corporation), or someone separate from the user group (e.g., a foundation funding the project or a Board of Directors member). I use the terms stakeholder and constituent to encompass a wider variety of people who are involved in the design and use of that design. This can include users, clients (funders or not), members of the design team, people who are indirectly affected by the design such as neighbors or taxpayers, or governmental or corporate entities that impact the availability and allowed use of land, products, or tools incorporated into the design process. In gathering data from any of these groups to inform your design, you should include groups whose voices matter for the design itself. At times this could include conversations with experts about the structure, safety, and legal requirements for a building. But in figuring out the aesthetic, spatial, and even emotional desires and impacts of a design, the stakeholder group goes beyond experts.

The included stakeholders should be chosen carefully so that input maps directly onto the design question you're answering. If you want to know what kind of features a new waterpark should include, it is probably best to include people who would likely use the park. But you wouldn't stop there. You'd also likely include neighbors whose living room windows face the park and who would not want any features to be too noisy or so large that their view of the sky is blocked. You'd talk with city officials, funders, and water safety experts. But you probably would not need to talk with people who live far away and do not plan to use the water park. That is, unless the funding piece includes concerns about the use of taxpayer dollars. The point of this example is to stress that it is important to be thoughtful about who should be included in a sample of people who should inform the design. You don't want to create something that is missing a key set of stakeholder voices in the design process. You do want to include enough people from each stakeholder group to inform the design. How many people you should include is discussed later in this chapter.

In UX research, the process of deciding whom to include in any research to inform design is called stakeholder mapping (see https://lucidspark.com/blog/a-guide-to-stakeholder-mapping for a how-to and template to do this). Stakeholders are people who are affected by your design, though the degree of impact may vary in terms of influence on the project, direct and indirect engagement with the design, and even desire to offer input. People with a lot of influence and interest are likely to be prioritized as key stakeholders, but others may remain in the project as design iterations are shown and vetted.

We need to have a clear idea of the topics we want to focus on when we gather data from a sample of people that we think will represent the views of the larger population. In other words, we need to know what variables we're studying, and how best to translate those into survey and interview questions, or into other methods such as observation or content analysis. We also need to determine how many variables we want to impose from the get-go, and how much we want salient topics and variables to emerge from the research participants. In addition to these deliberations, we also need to think about how many people we'd like to include in our data collection, and why particular types of people may be included. We also need to think about whether we are able to gather the input of every person who may use a space, and whether we are able to gather input from users across time (including one user at a time) or all at the same time.

Sampling Techniques

A *sample* is a subset of a population that we include in a study in order to make claims about that population. Representativeness is crucial if we want to make claims that the data from our sample can be generalized to the larger population. If our sample is somehow unusual relative to the overall population, we may get some of our claims wrong. This matters for projects that involve hundreds of people and those that involve only a few. There are different types of samples of people included in socially-informed research. The type of sample depends on availability of people, goals of a project, and type of generalizability desired. The types of samples covered here include random, stratified, systematic, quota, judgment, convenience, and snowball. I also discuss multistage sampling.

Random sampling, which allows for statistical generalizability (because everyone in a population has an equal chance of being included in the research), can be achieved by drawing names out of a hat (for a small group), or by using a random number generator to pick people. This kind of sampling falls under the heading *probability sampling*. Probability sampling is good at preventing bias because it doesn't allow the values or wishes of the researcher (or possibly the client) to affect who gets included. Because everyone has an equal probability (or chance) of being selected, they also have a chance of not being selected. This means that any subgroup that interests a researcher may end up being excluded from the research. This is why *stratified random sampling*, where researchers pick a random sample within each of the subsets (or strata) that they want to be represented in the research, is often preferable. An example of stratified random sampling would be surveying a random sample of college athletes within each sport (and maybe even stratifying by gender) to ask their opinions when designing a new athletic facility.

Systematic sampling – for example, picking every tenth person on a list – is similar to random sampling and is considered to be a type of probability sampling, but may lack representativeness because of how a list of people may be organized. For example, if a list of people is arranged by home address and one person in every nth neighborhood is chosen, areas that are more densely populated will be numerically underrepresented.

Samples may be drawn that are not random. These are termed *non-probability samples* because people are not given an equal chance to be included in the research. Sometimes this occurs because a random sample is too difficult to get. In less-than-desirable research projects, it can also occur because a researcher or other powerful stakeholder in the research wants to exclude people from the research because their views may not be popular or support the goals of a person in power. But more often than not, a non-probability sample is collected based on some logic or goal of a project. The following are non-probability sampling techniques.

A *quota sample* occurs when researchers make sure that at least someone from each of any relevant stakeholder groups is included in the research, but the people chosen within the subgroups are chosen not by chance but by some other factors (e.g., availability, preference for inclusion by supervisors, interest in the project). This method can help ensure that enough people from all relevant groups are included. A quota is like a bucket that needs to be filled, where a research project includes several buckets that represent subgroups whose voices are helpful to include because they may engage with a design based on their specific group's roles or goals. This sampling technique ensures that a certain number of people within a group is achieved and that each group has the desired number of people. Groups do not need to have an equal number of people in them. Quota sampling does risk selection based on non-random factors (such as availability or likelihood to be seen as helpful by people who create the samples) which can bias results. But at least there are people from each group who are participating. An example of quota sampling is when a new elementary school is being designed and the designers gather input from 100 people, ensuring that at least 50 participants are students, 20 are teachers, 20 are parents, and 10 are administrators.

Even if subgroups are not needed, researchers can be purposive in their sampling, sometimes referred to as *judgment sampling*. This technique includes using researcher or stakeholder expertise and social connections to decide what types of people to include in the research. I liken this technique to an archeological dig wherein the researcher does not dig a thousand random holes in Kansas to find dinosaur bones; rather, she goes to the spot where she believes bones are likely to be found and digs a lot of holes in that spot. In design research, judgment sampling may be useful in projects where particular types of people are likely to use a space; for example, seeking the input of technology experts in the design of a new computer lab in a public library would be useful.

A common non-probability sampling technique is *convenience sampling* (which can include judgment sampling). Researchers include participants who are convenient to reach, either because they are available and interested, or they are the ones whom researchers are able to contact. While convenience sampling is common, it does run the risk of being non-representative. This is because a researcher's network or the population of people who are available and interested in participating are likely not representative of the whole population who'd engage with a design once it's done. One version of convenience sampling is *snowball sampling* – when people who participate in the research are asked to "spread the word" about the research and help identify (and sometimes contact) others who may be eligible and interested in participating. The sample thus "snowballs" out from a core group of original participants to a bigger sample. The same concerns about representativeness (and generalizability) remain with snowball sampling.

Realistically, socially-informed research in design will include different types of sampling, each occurring at different stages in the design process. This is called *multistage sampling*. For example, in early stages, an organization's leadership team may inform designers of the goals of a project. After initial designs are rendered, a quota sample of employees across various roles, statuses, and physical locations may be asked to participate and offer feedback. After a design is completed and the space has been used for several weeks or months, a survey of people who enter the space could provide insights about small improvements that could be made.

As you can see, even figuring out who is included in a design research project is a complicated puzzle. One of the main things to think about is whether the design process necessitates including people who are reluctant to speak out or who may not be able to access or see an invitation to participate as possible in the first place. Socially-informed research must be attentive to inclusivity, and to taking as many steps as possible to allow for often invisible voices to be made visible. By doing this, designs will continue to be useful and helpful for all people.

Sample Size

We can't gather input from every single potential resident or user involved in every single design project. An important goal in any research is to gather input from people who, when observed or asked, would show or tell an accurate story about the larger population of people who may inhabit any design (or who, when added together, would tell an accurate story about the population of people who may inhabit that type of design). My students always find it fascinating to learn that, as long as relevant demographic characteristics of a subgroup of the population that you're studying such as race, region, age, and income are proportional to the whole US population, you don't really need to survey more than a couple of thousand people to capture the pulse of the entire country. This is because after a certain number of people are included in a large-scale quantitative survey project, a researcher's confidence that the data is representative doesn't necessarily increase with larger numbers.

But does a sample need to include thousands of people? My students also find it fascinating that I have published research articles based on sample sizes of no more than a couple dozen interviewees. In these cases, my aim was not to generalize to an entire population but to study a new topic to get at the deeper meaning and details about people's experiences that had not yet been studied. I aimed to test some concepts with a small group, which would allow other researchers to use those concepts and test them with a larger sample to see if the patterns held beyond the small and relatively homogeneous group of people in my study. Sometimes, then, representativeness is less crucial if we are aiming to study something new, especially if we think that what we're studying may be experienced similarly across groups. For projects where the population is the entire set of people working in an organization, a design project may include the participation of a few people just to get started with the preliminary ideas of the project but then ensure representativeness later on when multiple stakeholder-specific needs are addressed in the design.

Identifying the people who should be invited to offer input into a design is both a simple and complex process – simple because it is not too hard to think about who ultimately will inhabit or use the design; complex because sometimes the users are not the only ones in a list of "who's who" that should offer input. In addition, in order for people to be included in the research, you have to think of them as being included and you have to be able to access them (and they have to actually participate). Even if you get access to all the groups that interest you, it can be challenging to figure out if you have included enough people across the groups.

The steps involved in figuring out who will be included in the part of your design project where you gather input from users, clients, and/or other stakeholders are as follows:

- First, think about all of the groups that should be included and write them down.
- Second, decide if these groups should offer their input separately from each other or in a group with multiple stakeholders present at the same time (if you do a survey, remember that you can send everyone the same survey but separate out responses by group).
- Third, note whether you are including input from one person on one project as part of a larger project of research that captures your design portfolio over time, and, if so, then assess whether there are any characteristics of this person that make them seem similar or different to others who have been part of your entire portfolio of this type of design project.
- Fourth, once you figure out which types of people should be involved and whether they'll offer input individually or collectively, and once you know whether all input will be collected in the timeframe of one project or over the course of several projects, the next step is to figure out how many people is enough. This fourth step is the subject of the next section on sample size.

Part of your task is to figure out which stakeholder groups to include. But how many people should you include? In a project where the client is the user and it is contained within a very small group of people (e.g., in a private home or small business), suffice it to say that your sample size should probably be as many people who are in the location as possible. In this case, your sample would be nearly the same as your population – everyone who will use the space is included in the research part of the design process. But in most cases, a design is meant for more than a tiny group of people. In those cases, how many people to include is important to consider.

UX expert Jakob Nielsen (2000) has said "5 is enough," which means that for any decision in the process of designing something new, you can make the decision with the input of five people. But it is important to note that this number is reserved for particular decisions where a quick "test" suffices. Some parts of the design process necessitate larger samples, while some only require a handful of people. Let's say you're assessing whether the placement of a workstation near a window will work for a tech company. You ask five people who'd be likely to work in that space to test this workstation placement and offer feedback via interviews. After three users, it becomes apparent that the glare from the nearby window will be a problem for work space visibility, and that the height of the desk would only accommodate people taller than six feet tall. You would not need to ask a dozen more people to give input on this stage of the design. You'd take these five people's experiences and revise the placement and height of the workstation. This is fast and accounts for obvious or high-frequency problems without needing to bother others at this stage of the design process (Sauro 2013).

On the other hand, if you need a small margin of error or want to get input on details that may affect different stakeholder groups differently (especially if there is a severe problem with a design), then you need to include many more people in the data-gathering process (Biddle 2020). In most cases, the input from many more people with assurance that each needed stakeholder group is represented is a better choice. And while within each group it may be that having five people give input is enough, even that cannot guarantee that a design will be usable or enjoyable by everyone. There are also particular data-gathering methods where statistical significance may be required (e.g., in quantitative analysis of survey or observational data) or where a funder or owner or client may need more compelling evidence in order to move forward with a design. After all, if you want better evidence for a change in workstation placement, it may be a bit more convincing to a client who has to pay for new furniture and labor to move it to say that 15 out of the full set of 20 employees want a desk by the window, rather than to say that three out of four people who happened to be asked want this.

Deciding how many people to include in research is a matter of deciding whether breadth or depth is more useful to inform future design. This isn't just a case of quantity over quality, because even quantitative studies with large sample sizes still need to be able to offer high-quality interpretations of patterns. Really, the sample size is a matter of the importance of representativeness. What does it mean to be representative? It means that you are confident that the people you've included in your sample – whether it is three people or 300 people – tell the story of the entire group of people involved in the project. If you are able to include most people in your data collection efforts, you can be pretty confident their responses represent the collective. But if you have only a few people included who represent the large group along important factors (and you are sure they do), then your sample may be just as representative. And even if you sense that the people included are offering highly idiosyncratic responses, the responses may point to patterns that warrant further study, and/or they may point to individual needs that, if met, would help everyone (which is the cornerstone of universal design). If you've heard the phrase "anecdotal evidence," you know it is often used as a way of saying "we don't have a representative sample and so we need to be tentative about our claims about the entire group." That's a helpful interpretation, and we do need to be cautious about making claims about a group when only a tiny portion of the group has spoken. But we also don't want to lose sight of the importance of individual needs and ideas that emerge from a tiny portion of a population that may meet collective needs or point to a need for more data collection.

If we include five people in our assessment of a work space design near a window, and all five of them happen to be people who have dozens of devices that require USB and electrical outlets (but most people who work in the organization do not), then we'd know that their views about where to locate outlets (and how many) may not be representative of the whole organization. So, in this case, we'd want to stratify our sample by the level of requirement of outlets, and then make sure we have a few people in each level included in any input session. Otherwise, the input from the handful of outlet-mongers would lead to the inclusion of too many outlets for the larger group of people working in that space.

To Whom It May Concern: Communicating with Participants via Invitations, Reminders, Incentives, and Thank Yous

While the rules for proper communication etiquette seem to change every time a new digital messaging platform is introduced into the marketplace, it is important to consider the format and content of communications with people whose input you are seeking throughout the design process, whether they are funders, clients, or users. Of course, how you communicate with people on the design team also matters, but that is something that varies depending on workplace culture and professional norms; this section is more about how designers communicate with people who are providing input but who are not on the design team. It is important to create appropriate and effective resident or user engagement strategies. This means that thinking about how to reach, include, and follow up with people is as important as the input they provide once they're involved.

Socially-informed research requires that the research is inclusive and that it is conducted in such a way that people want to participate and feel as if their input counts. For this reason, how people are invited to participate matters quite a bit. People want to have their voices included. If they are suspicious of the means for gathering input, of the motivation for gathering input, or even of the amount of effort that they perceive organizational leaders are putting into the input-gathering, they will be reluctant to participate. If they are required to participate as part of their work, that adds a layer of complexity in terms of their investment in the process, their willingness to be honest, or their belief that they actually have a say in any work decisions.

If you are already working with clients, you have likely established patterned ways to communicate with them. If your organization is small, you may be directly connecting with clients via text, email, or phone. For larger organizations or projects, you may be part of a team where one person serves as the communication point person with the client. In either case, the way we talk with clients is part of the larger *culture* – the established way of doing things that demonstrate the larger values of the group participating – of the design project itself. That's why it's important to explicitly assess existing communication patterns, determine if they're working, and then use effective communication mechanisms to seek participation (and recommendations for other stakeholders to participate) in data collection.

Accessing people to offer input in the design process can usually start with the users themselves. The clients funding or initiating the project will often know whose input should be included, but they should not be the only place to look to ensure you have included input from all of the necessary constituencies. You or other stakeholders may know who else needs to be included. How people are identified to participate in the research process is itself a social process. This identification and invitation require the researchers to understand motivation, incentives, and effective ways to communicate why input matters.

People need reminders and they need to feel as if their input is helpful. For this reason, socially-informed research should include an explicit plan and division of labor for the design team to (a) clearly and inclusively invite participants, (b) use communication forms and channels that are already effective within an organization to recruit and remind participants of input-gathering sessions, and (c) and offer gratitude to participants for their input, either in the session itself or through follow-up communication. Some people say that handwritten notes are preferred if you want to show your gratitude, possibly because, as my own research (Janning 2018) shows, they connote making an effort and taking time to express gratitude rather than sending a digital mass message. However, I think it's safe to say that preferred communication that is meant to convey gratitude and thoughtfulness can look different depending on the age of the recipient, the communication norms of an organization, or the capacity of a design group to convey gratitude to a large group of people (depending on the scale of the input-gathering process). What matters more than communication format is THAT the communication of gratitude occurs. This is especially crucial at multiple points in the design process so that participants can feel motivated and called to continue participating over time and as the design gets refined and shown for more feedback. The deeper and longer the investment from people who offer input, the more likely the design will meet the widest array of needs from users.

It used to be that the reward for participating in any kind of data-gathering in a design project was simply the experience of participation itself, and the knowledge that a design is informed by participants. But as projects turn more toward engaging with communities before and during the design process, the time and commitment from participants have not only become more important but have also grown in scale. Because of this, it is more common to hear stories about research participants receiving monetary compensation for their time. For example, Homage Hospitality co-founder Damon Lawrence (2022), in a presentation at the 2022 Hospitality Design Conference, noted that he now compensates stakeholders – especially neighborhood residents – whose voices inform the design of hotels his team is building. This is important, he argues, because he is African-American and many of the communities where his businesses reside are made up predominantly of this population – a population that has been harmed by past research processes that have ranged from extracting information to actual physical and psychological harm. It is because of past harms that social scientists have focused on the significance of monetary compensation for participation in research (after informed consent is secured) as an ethical issue. For too long those in power have been able to extract ideas (sometimes in the form of data) from people who have less of a say in the design process, at times only to be able to give a cursory and superficial nod to consultation. Needless to say, extracting data from people who are not in powerful positions in the design process (or in the world) without proper thanks or compensation, and extracting it only for the optics of inclusion, are not practices of socially-informed research. In sociological research, compensation should match the effort it may have taken for someone to participate. This means that if someone had to take time out of a paid work day to offer input in the design process (which is particularly difficult for hourly or shift workers with little vacation time), they should be compensated accordingly. Or, if participation is expected by people who work for an organization that is designing a new space, there should be no expectation that they participate outside of their usual paid work schedule (nor penalized if they opt not to participate since nobody should ever be forced to participate in research).

People who participate in research need to understand why they are doing so, and how their input will be used (and by whom). A lot of designers – especially those who see themselves invested in human-centered design specifically – would say that storytelling is a key ingredient in the design process. As data is collected from people and design ideas are iterated and shared, designers and architects need to be able to use the data to inform the design story being told to involved stakeholders. Because of this, part of the communication process has to include ways to tell audiences not just what you are designing and why, but how you will use (and have used) their input to get to those design decisions. Transparency is a key element of socially-informed research in the design process, and the iterative design path must thus include moments when the data story is part of the design story.

The next section elaborates on how and why a socially-informed research process matters in design in terms of inequality and power. This relates to communication because socially-informed research necessitates that people feel included in any invitation to participate, that their voices matter, and that they are aware of how that input will be gathered and used.

Who Has the Power? How Inequalities and Power Matter in Research

My brother Dr. Marty Janning, who is an ear, nose, and throat surgeon, has shared with me on more than one occasion that his input on the technical and health-related specifics (including the precise temperature of the space) of an operating room were crucial when he and his partners were working with an architecture firm to design their new clinic. But he also noted that staff members in his clinic besides the surgeons likely have a better grasp on how a space may be more or less conducive to patient privacy and comfort in areas such as the waiting room or hallways. When I spoke with architect Romano Nickerson about his work on designing health care settings, he highlighted the importance of being able to talk with not only physicians, but also with people in every role in order to get a feel for how the day-to-day tasks and use of space actually play out. Collecting data from stakeholders with varied statuses and "say" in the design process is not only more democratic, it tells the designers (and maybe even the organization itself) how its organizational hierarchy may shape the design.

If you design a research study, you are, in effect, a gatekeeper of who gets to be included, what questions they get asked, and how their input is studied and packaged to inform future design (or to report back to the client). The client who hires you is also a gatekeeper. Socially-informed design requires inclusion of all voices that matter in any design. This may include unpopular voices, or voices of people a client may wish to exclude. Gone are the days of designing with no attention to the needs and desires of a diverse set of stakeholders. While the designers (and yes, often the funders) have a loud voice in the design process, a design will work better if it includes the ideas from those who otherwise may not have a chance to chime in. In fact, the move toward more socially-informed design suggests that community and stakeholder input is no longer seen as a hoop to jump through, but rather a crucial element in informing good design that actually meets the needs of those who will engage with that design over time. To be socially sustainable in design is as crucial as being environmentally sustainable, and the recognition of power and inequality in the design process itself needs to be part of that sustainability.

I've been involved in the creation of a human-centered design program at my institution. Part of the discussion around this term has included the group asking ourselves "which humans?" By that we mean to say that we have to pay attention to how design can exacerbate inequalities in our world. It can do this by ignoring the voices of those who have less opportunity to chime in. Or it can do this by including people but failing to recognize that people come to the design table with different amounts of cultural capital. Cultural capital, as I defined in the Introduction, is the social, material, and even linguistic resources someone has that make others see them as having higher status, which, in turn, brings them even more resources. If someone has less cultural capital than others, they may not have the confidence to share their ideas if they are intimidated by the vocabulary, tone of voice, or demographic traits of others in the group being asked to give feedback.

Socially-informed design requires putting into place process pieces that allow designers to take a step back and make sure that all voices that should be included in any feedback process are included. This means that asking for ideas about which groups to invite for feedback should go beyond the funder and beyond clients who are the most powerful people in an organization. There should be explicit inclusion of moments in the input-gathering process to ensure everyone has a chance to give their input. If all design was based only on the louder voices, the needs of those people with quieter (literally and figuratively) voices would go unmet.

Socially-informed design also requires transparency. If people who are asked to offer input in the design process understand why they're being asked certain questions or placed in certain scenarios, they'll feel more comfortable participating. More comfort yields a greater likelihood for them to trust you as designers and input-gatherers. It follows, then, that their responses to your questions will be more honest, possibly more thorough, and more likely to include creative ideas. If we feel at all unfamiliar with people or a situation, it takes time for us to figure out what's going on, what our role is, and whether we can trust the process and the people facilitating that process. If we know what's going on, we can skip ahead to the fun part of offering input and informing the design with honest ideas.

One way that transparency operates in formal social science research is through *informed consent*. This process entails researchers offering potential participants a verbal or written narrative explaining the risks and benefits of participating in the research, researcher contact information or support resources in case the research is troubling or traumatic, and the opportunity for the participant to skip any part of the research or opt out entirely. It is also the place where the subject of the research is described. So, for example, when I conducted interviews with second homeowners about their vacation homes, I asked them to sign an informed consent document where I explained my topic in a general way (how homeowners and their families use and define their second homes) and I noted risks and benefits (sometimes it can be hard to talk about family memories, but most people find discussing their homes and family experiences to be a pleasant experience). The form said they could opt out of any questions, although nobody refused to answer any of my interview questions throughout the process.

For most of your work in socially-informed research, you would be unlikely to include a formal informed consent document for people who provide input to read and sign. When I served as a consultant on design projects, the transparency occurred in other ways. Namely, the architects and designers would helpfully explain why they were collecting the type of input they were collecting, what our input would inform, and how our past input had informed the current iteration of the design. In these meetings, it was also often the case that organizational leaders and people managing the budget would also explain any limitations to the ideas shared. Thus, while none of us signed any official informed consent documents, we understood what we were getting into, and how our words and ideas would be used by others. Presumably, this not only provides an ethical approach to a design project, it also makes people who offer input feel as if their ideas and experiences matter. If people feel as if they matter, the design is clearly socially-informed.

References

Biddle, Toby. 2020. "Why 5 UX Testers Are Almost Never Enough." Loop11, September 10. https://www.loop11.com/why-5-ux-testers-are-almost-never-enough/.

Janning, Michelle. 2018. *Love Letters: Saving Romance in the Digital Age*. In the Routledge Series for Creative Teaching and Learning in Anthropology (The Anthropology of Stuff). New York: Routledge.

Lawrence, Damon. 2022. "HDAC Series: Holistic Wellbeing and Community by Design." Panel Presentation at the Hospitality Design Expo and Conference. Las Vegas, April 27.

Lucas, Ray. 2016. *Research Methods for Architecture*. London: Laurence King Publishing.

Nielsen, Jakob. 2000. "Why You Only Need to Test with 5 Users." Nielsen Norman Group, March 18. https://www.nngroup.com/articles/why-you-only-need-to-test-with-5-users/.

Sauro, Jeff. 2013. "5 Reasons You Should and Should Not Test with 5 Users." MeasuringU, December 13. https://measuringu.com/five-for-five/.

Setting and Pace for Data Collection – The WHERE and WHEN

4

I have interviewed and worked with interior designers and architects across the world. I've also worked on projects that are fast remodels, and some that required years of planning and research before implementing. Some of my projects are in limbo because they got going before the pandemic and then had to halt as a result of all of the global changes in resources, community connectedness, and public health concerns. Where the projects have been located has also been influenced by these factors, even before COVID-19. Our social world is impacted by place and time; where we live and the historical period (and even our own age) affect how we experience the world, including the built environment and its furnishings. The elements of place and time have been an important part of the story of every design. Without understanding where and when a design is created or used, we can't fully understand the motivation or impact of that design.

In this chapter, I delve into my own research about the significance of place, setting, and time in understanding social relations. Since gathering data is, in itself, a social relationship between the researchers and the clients/users, and since much of the data gathered will connect directly to the impact of spaces and material dimensions contained within those spaces, it is especially important to discuss how the place in which the data is gathered may matter. Time also matters in terms of the data gathering itself (e.g., How long should it take someone to fill out a survey? What happens if the interviewee talks for a long time? What if your clients offer feedback one at a time over a period of several months?). It also matters in terms of planning a project, which includes thinking about what matters in pre- and post-tests and setting up a realistic calendar for the various methods introduced in Chapter 2.

Where and When Does the Design Go? Geographic, Cultural, and Temporal Contexts

Socially-informed research in the design process must take into consideration geographic and cultural context. Whether it's the use of local building materials or local communities' ordinances about what is allowed to be built, place matters. I have lived and studied in four different countries, and in each place, I have paid attention to the ways that my engagement with designed spaces is shaped by the cultural context. When I studied in South Africa in 1994, just prior to the first post-Apartheid democratic national election, I learned how neighborhood and township demarcations by race shaped not only what sorts of household products and decor items people used and displayed, but also how residents had variable access to public transportation, groceries, and clean water. When I walked up six flights of steps to my apartment in Denmark in 2012 I couldn't help but think about how country-specific building codes can affect access to spaces depending on people's physical capacities.

I have lived in locations that range from a town with 5,000 inhabitants (where I grew up) to a city with more than two million residents. Urban–rural differences in design take shape in obvious ways: skyscrapers in the city, silos in the country. But beyond these differences, it has also become apparent to me that lifestyles, modes of transportation, and views about land use and privacy vary from place to place, and are essential to consider when designing spaces. When I lived in an urban area, I had to allow more time for a commute, regardless of whether I took my own car or used public transportation. In the small town where I grew up, I drove a lot of places but it only took a few minutes to get anywhere. The pace of life was a bit slower. In the city, people lived close together and it was not surprising to see people walking around in their pajamas in a dense apartment building with the curtains open, whereas doing this in my hometown, where the dwellings were spread farther apart, would have felt awkward. And certainly, in places where there is less room for expansion (and maybe even less room for in-fill), the plan to build a one-story sprawling school would be met with raised eyebrows (and probably ordinances that disallow spread in dense neighborhoods). Finally, where I grew up in southwestern Minnesota bordered the Lower Sioux Native American reservation. This meant that I was raised with an understanding of the significance of history on how people thought about place. We did not have formal land acknowledgments in our daily lives in the 1970s and 1980s about the indigenous ancestry of land that had been conquered and exploited by white settlers, but the notion that land meant something different for different groups was an explicit part of my upbringing.

In the US, unequal access to space, natural resources, and control over the meaning of place has been formed through a long history of racism, sexism, classism, and colonialism. Even the term "homeowner" has excluded women, people of color, and many immigrant groups in the history of our country. Whether one can decorate one's own dwelling, let alone afford to hire a designer or architect, shapes the meaning of place for that person. Control over space, usually in the form of owning that space, is not required in order for someone to attach meaning to the space (for example, even someone who is incarcerated may attach meaning to spaces in a prison). But control does play a big role in someone's ability to alter, sell, or inherit that space.

Socially-informed research requires us to recognize that wherever a design is placed, local customs, values, and ways of life must inform that design. Whether it's a hospital located in a country where value is placed on technological intervention or one in a place where excessive technology is viewed as an inhibitor to natural mother–child bonding, place affects not only what people believe, but how spaces and objects are designed and used.

I have spent the better part of two decades studying the importance of spaces and places in our understanding of human social behavior. Our roles and relationships are "placed" – they do not exist just in our heads. They change depending on where we are. In my 2017 book *The Stuff of Family Life* (Janning 2017), as I move through the chapters I move from room to room in a home and describe what we know about real family lives today that may relate to the functions of each room. I detail how the particular room (and its décor and objects) helps tell the story of one aspect of contemporary family life. Some examples of today's family stories that are found in the book's "home tour" include

- Findings of my survey research on what people do with their digital and paper love letters by discussing the bedroom – its history, its place as a private space within a private home, and as a location for keeping intimate secrets close and safely preserving values we attach to romantic love.
- Survey findings of college students' conceptions of home as they move from a childhood home to a college dorm room, and then to an imagined future adult home. In these findings, I reveal that the control over space (and its contents) is a marker of adult identity that we often forget in research on the transition to adulthood. In another chapter, I highlight interview research on how young adults whose parents divorce often use their bedroom spaces (and technology) in two homes in ways that demonstrates the closeness they feel to either parent.

- Interview research results that show how people's management of the boundary between paid work and home life can be seen in the use of objects and spaces. Patterns in the interviews included decisions about whether to bring work laptops into the bedroom, use of the commute to transition from a home self to a work self (and vice versa), and some people's capacity to do paid work and personal activities in the exact same space, thus not necessitating a separate home office.

It probably goes without saying that most interior designers and architects already know that places matter in our consideration of people's roles and relationships. Consider how the COVID-19 pandemic changed the way people think about their homes and work spaces, whether it's turning a dining room into a home office for telecommuting, or adding a fire bowl to a patio to have social gatherings outside. Consider also how even painting one wall a different color can feel like the room is suddenly filled with our personalities. Or, consider how a remodel of an office space from a sea of cubicles to a more open and changeable set of work spots can change the frequency and type of interactions between colleagues. Spaces become places when they are given meaning. Sometimes the designs themselves create that meaning, as when a restaurant meant to give off a feel for a particular geographic region may contain colors and objects from that region. But sometimes the inhabitants of a space revise or redefine the meaning by adding their own personal touch. Whether it's placing special mementos in a living room of a memory care facility or rearranging furniture to create conversation spaces rather than media viewing spaces, spaces become places when they have meaning that matters to their inhabitants and users. It is every designer and architect's job to pay attention to that meaning for the people who occupy the spaces and for the communities surrounding them.

I have also conducted research that wrestles with our understanding of time. As a sociologist, I pay attention to how time is socially constructed. We decide what constitutes being on time or late; we figure out how much time we think is needed to do certain tasks; and some groups punish people who may not fit into their accepted rules and norms about time. With the previously mentioned example of research on work and home boundaries, I also included interview questions about how people may divide up their time into segments that could be easily (or not-so-easily) classified as "work" or "personal/family" time. Just as people had to pivot during the pandemic to figure out how home spaces were suddenly supposed to be work and school spaces, too, the time spent in homes changed drastically. For some people, crowded calendars became sparsely filled, and for others there seemed to be not nearly enough time given the stresses and work that accompanied a global health crisis. Additionally, because of historical influences on social patterns, time matters for how people use design and it matters for the design process itself.

The next sections take place and time in turn, with a focus on how they matter sociologically and on how they matter in the design process.

Where Should the Research Take Place? On-site versus Off-site, Location-Based Methods, and Public/Private Boundaries

As part of my research on the social meaning of second homes (both investment properties and vacation homes) a few years ago, I was able to do many of the interviews in person in the homes of the interviewees (Janning 2019). The interview questions focused on how homeowners understood their second home as meaningful in terms of connectedness with family or neighbors, or in terms of economic benefit to themselves or their communities (or both). Because the participants were from all over the country, I got to explore lots of new neighborhoods. From the affluent ski towns of Vail, Colorado to the quiet lakefronts in central Minnesota, and from the mid-century homes in Palm Springs to the cabins along the Oregon Coast, I became an expert in following audio navigation in whatever rental car I was in. I was glad I lived in a time when I did not need to endanger myself by looking at a map at the same time I paid attention to the details of the neighborhoods (though I do like pulling over and studying maps in new places). I would often arrive early to someone's neighborhood, in which case I would drive around and then park a block away so I could take quick notes (often on a notes app on my phone that I would then email to myself) about what I had just seen, heard, and noticed. Sometimes I would also take pictures of public places so that when I wrote about my research findings, I could jog my memory about the places my interviewees talked about. My notes included details about architectural styles, distances between buildings, types of landscapes and hardscapes, activities people were doing, and the types (and names) of commercial spaces nearby. I was also able to visit neighborhoods of interviewees with whom I had only been able to talk on the phone. In those cases, I pulled out the interview transcripts and did my best to find the places they talked about. With my adventures in new neighborhoods filled with new sites and sounds that offered richness to the stories told by my interviewees, I started realizing that my interview project was helped by my detailed and in-depth observations of the geographic and spatial context of the homes. I dubbed this part of my research a "rental car ethnography."

Ethnography is an in-depth observational study of a group of people, often in a particular location over time or surrounding an event, where the observer may blend in or keep themselves separate from the goings-on at the site (or anywhere in between these). The researcher takes lots of field notes – either handwritten or typed into a digital device, and sometimes audio recorded – about what they see, hear, taste, smell, and touch, including any observations about what people in the setting are doing or saying that can be overheard in a public setting. In sociology, as cited in our professional ethics statement, as long as we are in a publicly-accessible place, we are able to conduct this kind of field research without people necessarily knowing; otherwise, we need to get permission from people involved in the situation we are observing. At regular moments in time, the researcher then reads over the field notes, making notations about patterns and connections that the notes reveal. For example, after a slow drive through one neighborhood on the Oregon Coast in my second homes study, I was able to map the locations of tsunami warning signs that interviewees referenced as they discussed their involvement with local volunteer opportunities (in that case, tsunami-preparedness groups).

As I drove around multiple neighborhoods and communities, I thought about an ethnographic research project I had done several years before the second homes project. It was an observational study I did at the building site of a home remodeling TV show (Janning 2008). In that project, my handwritten field notes included maps of the site, observations of tools used, colors worn, work tasks completed, shifts between on- and off-screen conversations, and even the way audience members watching the filming looked at those of us in the "VIP" tent. Of course, I also noted any sightings of the celebrity hosts of the show.

As I continued with the second homes project, it became clear to me that use of homes for both income and pleasure was not uncommon. This led me to an ethnographic project at a conference for vacation rental homeowners, during which I took notes about anything related to framing vacation homes as "good for communities," "good for families," or "good for income." Importantly, if people started talking with me at the conference, I noted that I was a researcher. But most of what I observed was in open sessions with a presenter and audience, where my role was not necessarily known to others. Because I was at a conference where people were taking notes about what they were learning, my note-taking about audience responses, speaker tone of voice, or visual displays that contained certain vivid messages about vacation rental properties did not look suspicious. I remember feeling exhilarated as I frantically tried to jot down every detail about what I was seeing and hearing, with occasional in-the-moment notes in the margins about what I thought it meant. As I looked back on my field notes when writing about my research findings, I was so glad I included the details from the conference (and from my rental car ethnography) about spaces, objects, and how people used both to communicate certain types of messages. Not only did the notes jog my memory of an event or a place, but they also helped me contextualize what my interviewees told me about their experiences and decisions. Their words and ideas were "placed" – situated geographically and spatially and thus made more vivid for me as I tried to uncover patterns in the interview data.

All of these details about my ethnographic experiences are meant to highlight the importance of place and setting in our understanding of people's roles and relationships. Our understanding is dependent on how well we are able to gather useful data about people's experiences. Since gathering data is, in itself, a social relationship between the researchers and the clients/residents, and since much of the data gathered will connect directly to the impact of spaces and material dimensions contained within those spaces, it is especially important to discuss how the place in which the data is gathered may matter. This is particularly important for design professionals whose work is "placed" in our physical world.

The next sections detail how specific types of spaces and data-gathering techniques that take place within certain spaces can be used in socially-informed research in design projects.

When you are hired by a person or organization to design a space, it matters if you are creating a design from the start or if you are redesigning an existing space. If you are redesigning a space, you would spend a lot of time on site figuring out what modifications you will be making. Likely you (and your entire team) would frequently meet the client or user on site to talk about ways the current space is not meeting their needs. And even for projects that are new builds, you would likely meet up with the client or user on site at least once or twice before the build to assess everything from potential views to traffic flows on the streets aligning the property. Once the design turns into a construction project, then on-site work expands and occurs more frequently.

Certainly, a lot of design work occurs off site, even if there are points in time when measurements, planning meetings, and data gathering occur at the site of the design. Some of the decisions about where to work on the design are necessitated by logistical requirements such as meeting with electrical inspectors, taking measurements, and assessing excavation. And if a designer is not in the same geographic location as the site, then geographic distance can lessen the flexibility for on-site work (or for clients or users to come to a designer's studio or workplace). I've worked with plenty of architects and designers where I never once visited their workplaces, because we did not live in the same town, because the parts of the design process with which I was involved required on-site meetings with multiple stakeholders, or because the designers knew that coming to us would allow them to gain a better understanding of our community. We trusted the designers because they took the time to come to us and really get a feel for the place where a new building would need to meet social and physical needs and complement existing buildings on site. Thus, beyond practical or logistical variables, some decisions about where to do research in the design process are based on social and methodological factors that include access to users and users' behaviors, the establishment of trust between clients and designers, and even people's values concerning privacy and confidentiality. I elaborate each of these factors below.

Access

In socially-informed research during the design process, designers will collect data from various stakeholders. Unless you're only using survey or phone/video call interview data (where you don't have to be physically in the same space as people participating in the research), you have to find a way to connect in person. Accessing users is a key component of data gathering, and it is necessary to be present in a designed space (or existing space that needs to be redesigned) to observe the use of the space and ask users questions about their attitudes and experiences. In most cases, this involves going to users, and not the other way around.

Trust

In addition to the convenience for users and the need to include data about actual use and engagement with a design, going to the site of the design can establish trust. This occurs in both directions: users and clients trust you because you have made an effort and taken time to come to their space, thus building your capacity to empathize with their experience; and you trust users and clients because you are better able to understand the context in which they are making decisions and expressing opinions. Putting it a bit crassly, whose turf you are on can shape the relationships. If clients or users feel like they are not on their own turf (as would happen if they only offered input at your place of business), they may feel less comfortable and relaxed. They may feel intimidated. Or, at the very least, they may have a hard time sharing ideas about a design or redesign if they can't point to the actual spaces and objects in their own setting that are informing their views.

Public and Private Spaces

Design projects can vary not only in terms of scope and scale but also in terms of whether the spaces being designed or redesigned are public or private. Gathering in-person interview data from passersby for a proposed playground is a public data-gathering process. So is making observations in a public place to get a feel for how people's current use may shed light on needed design improvements. Contrastingly, gathering input from patients and staff in a proposed clinic design is more private (especially if the disclosure of medical conditions is part of the research). If data is being collected in a public setting or for a public place, then the research does not need to include as much attention to ensuring confidentiality. Designers who are visible on site and visibly gather input from people not only make the entire design project more public, but they also need to think about what clients or users may desire in terms of disclosing their views on the design. As I discussed in Chapter 3, confidentiality is one of the most common considerations in conducting ethical research. The more public the setting, the less confidential people's views are and the less hidden the design project is from passersby. The more private the setting, the greater the likelihood that confidentiality will matter.

Even within the setting where the design is taking place, there are different types of spaces that can affect how research works in the design process. Some of this has to do with privacy and status, which connects to confidentiality. If people of differing statuses are included in the data-gathering process, and if these individuals fear some kind of retaliation from superiors if they express their views, then it is crucial to offer private settings for them to share what they're thinking. In addition to you assuring them that their views will be confidential and that their identities will not be disclosed, you also need to set up data-gathering spaces that allow for this to occur. If you do research on-site, find places with doors or curtains that close so that visual and auditory clues about people's views are not available to anyone besides you. Normally, design projects would not include extreme situations of mistrust or power differentials within an organization or community, but you'd be surprised how much people's fear of what others think of them shapes what they're willing to disclose. Designers asking people for their views should set up spaces and data-gathering techniques that allow for honesty and comfort. As you can imagine, the spaces in which the data-gathering takes place can play a role in how comfortable people are in sharing their honest views.

When Should You Collect Data? Timing and Pace in Data Collection

When I talked with Lori Bettison-Varga, the Natural History Museum (NHM) of Los Angeles County President and Director, she shared a story about the importance of time in conducting socially-informed research in the design process. This was in the context of a space that they are developing called the NHM Commons, which will be an indoor-outdoor design that includes exhibits alongside spaces for community events, leisure activities, and ways to symbolically and psychologically connect people with the natural world. While the partners in the design process have used community members' input to formulate initial designs, they also include planning for further community connections as the process unfolds. As Lori described,

> Everyone should be able to call this their place. Ultimately the goal is to show that we are a museum of, for, and with Los Angeles. This doesn't just happen. We need to develop community partnerships and co-sponsor activities now to lay the groundwork, to make it viable. We can't just create it and expect people to show up.

In order for people to want to feel a sense of belonging in a place and, thus, to actually use the space in ways it was meant to be used (especially a large civic space such as the one the NHM is working on), they need to trust the people creating the space in the first place. They need to feel comfortable in the space. This kind of relationship-building takes time. And time, as any sociological researcher will tell you, is crucial to consider carefully when thinking about data collection, analysis, and sharing in the design process.

For most projects, designers and architects need to consider how much time they would spend (and how often) with people who will eventually be managing or using the space. How much people will be engaging with the design once built also matters. There is also variation in how much time there is between completion of a project and any *post-occupancy evaluation* (POE) (which is defined as research conducted after a design is completed to see if the goals of the design are being met). Timing matters in terms of planning a project, which includes thinking about what matters in pre- and post-tests, and setting up a realistic calendar for the various methods introduced in Chapter 2. When considering timing, it is also important to keep in mind that on-site and off-site check-ins can vary in their timing and frequency depending on the location and complexity of a project, and on the relationship a designer has with clients or users. The next few paragraphs delve into tips to keep in mind for frequency and timing of research in the design process.

In social science research, we distinguish between cross-sectional and longitudinal projects. Cross-sectional research involves data-gathering processes that occur in one moment in time or within a short amount of time. Of course, there is no such thing as instantaneous data (even short surveys stay open for a few days, and even a fast survey takes a little time to fill out), but it is safe to say that data collected in a short amount of time captures a snapshot of patterns that may or may not change over time. Survey projects that I've done where respondents are sent a link and then have a couple of weeks to respond are cross-sectional. Ethnographic projects where I've taken field notes on site for one day are cross-sectional. Even interview projects can be cross-sectional. In fact, I've done interview projects where I collected data from people once, but the full set of interviews took me a year to complete. In all of these cases, people are responding or being observed once, and at one moment in time.

Longitudinal research occurs over time. People who participate are part of the data collection process at more than one point in time. Sometimes this occurs at regular intervals, as with surveys or interviews that are conducted each year for a few years. Studying something longitudinally allows researchers to notice dynamic patterns that may change. Longitudinal research can occur regardless of whether you're collecting data from one person and project at a time, or from big groups of people who offer input at multiple points in time relating to one project. In quantitative social science research, there are numerous large national and international datasets of survey responses collected from people over many years, or even decades. These datasets are used to track whether large portions of the population have changed in terms of anything from religious views to educational outcomes. If the periodic check-ins occur with the same group of people, this is called a panel study. Some longitudinal research takes place almost constantly and for weeks or months at a time. Examples of this include projects where the researcher lives with or near a group of people being studied, often using extensive ethnographic field notes to capture daily activities that, when analyzed, may reveal patterns that seem to last a long time. It is possible to get quite in-depth with this kind of research.

Research in the design process can oscillate between cross-sectional and longitudinal research in complex ways. Many design projects include a series of several cross-sectional studies, where data is collected quickly at a few points in time. In these cases – let's say it's a study of how people use a new configuration of entrances and exits in a library – researchers may pick a handful of times to make observations over a multi-week period. This could be three or four one-hour sessions where the field notes may also reveal patterns that show behaviors that stay the same or that change. Or it could be a project where users of proposed designed spaces are surveyed before, during, and after the design process to see if their attitudes about the design changed during the design process itself. In these cases, the designation of them as purely cross-sectional or longitudinal matters less than the alignment of the timing and technique of data collection with the design research question.

Importantly, how long and how frequently data from clients, users, or other stakeholders should be varies depending on desired level of scientific precision, intended audience, and likelihood to publish results from the research or just use them to inform the design as it gets revised along the way. In UX (user experience) and human-centered design research, often used in tech companies and corporate design firms, precision matters to be sure, but taking too much time to collect robust data or fill a formal stratified random sample can delay the design process and cost time, money, and trust between designers and clients. While I was able to note some important patterns that I observed on the reality TV set I referenced earlier, I was only there for a day. It was not nearly enough time to gather salient patterns that could have led to a publication beyond just description of the experience. Really, I should have been there every day for at least a week, which is what I'd recommend to anyone who wants to establish empathy for end-users and other stakeholders before designing things for them.

Take a minute to think about what you would need to do to truly understand someone's life – their daily routines, movement paths, thought processes, moments of conflict or frustration, and interactions with others. It is hard to really understand someone's life if you only hang out with them for a day. But a week can offer at least a glimmer of reality. And doing this across seasons can be even more helpful if seasonal change affects behaviors. This is an important realization for ethnographers: spend enough time so that people you're observing or interacting with "get real," wherein they lower their inhibitions and lessen moments of acting or pretending to come across as favorable.

Figuring out how much time to spend gathering data from stakeholders in a design project requires a delicate balance – take enough time so people do not feel rushed, excluded due to low availability, or likely to perform a role that may not represent what they're usually like. But don't take so much time that project resources (and patience) are used up before a design is complete.

Below I offer a set of timing guidelines for data collection that falls somewhere between the required depth and rigor for formal social scientific research (aimed at publishing for an academic audience), and research done for efficient decision-making during a design project (as would be more likely to occur in applied sociology projects). I provide tips for each of the large methods categories introduced in Chapter 2, as well as for time-use studies (which I define more fully below).

Surveys

The amount of time you spend designing a survey will depend on the length of the survey and the complexity of the questions you're asking. If it's a 30-second pen-and-paper survey used to get fast feedback on a design mock-up, you could draft the survey relatively quickly. If it's a complex survey meant for multiple stakeholder groups that gets at several attitudinal measures, it will take longer – sometimes several weeks – to research good ways to ask a question, how to organize the questions, and set up the survey so analysis is manageable. The bottom line with any survey is to allow more time than you think to develop the questions, since, as I discussed in Chapter 2, asking questions in a way that is ethical and leads to good data is not easy. Once you administer a survey, I suggest that you leave it open for at least three days and preferably a week or two so that you can capture people whose work and other schedules make them more and less available on certain days to fill out a survey. If a survey is open for a week or more, it is useful to send reminders halfway through the collection time period (and not on a Friday or Saturday).

Interviews

As with surveys, how much time you spend designing an *interview guide* (the list of questions you'll ask, sometimes called an interview schedule or protocol) depends on how much detail and depth you want in people's responses, and how much input a client may want to offer. It also depends on how many people on your team (if you have a team) can do the interviews (which takes less time than one person conducting all interviews), and how many people you'd like to interview. Generally, it is a good idea to gather interview data within a month. I advise several sociology research projects for students each year, where they have about a month to collect and analyze data. For those who are conducting around 10–15 interviews that each last 30–60 minutes, 2–3 weeks to actually do the interviews seems to accommodate schedules (they and their interviewees have busy lives) and leaves another week or two for analysis. Unlike surveys, interviews do not automatically produce written responses to questions; transcription is necessary. Allow four to five times the amount of time an interview takes to transcribe it. This means if you do ten interviews that are each an hour long, you have ten hours of interview transcripts. It will take you 40–50 hours to transcribe these. If you use transcription software or outsource transcription to a paid service, allow at least the amount of time each interview took to review the transcripts for errors and prep them for analysis. Of course, for short interviews with fairly easy or quick responses, all of this time is shortened.

Ethnographic or Observational Research

Usually, this kind of research requires more than just a one-time session, since people's behaviors or paths of travel or schedules vary not only over the hours of a day, but also over the course of a week, month, or longer season. For this reason, if one of the goals of research is to get a detailed vision of what life is like for people who will eventually engage with a design, it is useful to have design team members spend at least a few days on site, making observations. This could be full days, or it could be parts of days where relevant patterns are most likely to be visible (e.g., how elevator use works at the start of the day, lunchtime, and end of the day).

Content Analysis

Data made up of text, images, or maps requires different amounts of time to collect, since some content analysis is done using existing content (e.g., published minutes of meetings), while other content has to be produced as part of the research process (e.g., asking users to map their usual daily movements in an office setting) and thus requires more time. The main tip I have with this method is to allow more time than you think you need if you want users or clients to create or produce the text, images, or maps that you'll use in your analysis. In some cases, you may ask people to chart or keep track of what they're doing, in which case it would require the amount of time that any observational analysis may require. It's just that people would be noting observations of their own day, rather than having someone else take the field notes.

Time-Use Studies

There are methods used in social science research that carry elements of the aforementioned methods with them, but which include the element of time as a more explicit feature. In general, people's memories are not that accurate, so surveys and interviews based on retrospective observations can be unreliable. For designers and architects who want to have a more accurate rendition of what people actually do (rather than just what they think they did), it can be helpful to use methods that require people to make note of what they're experiencing, doing, or thinking as it happens. These methods include *time-use studies or diaries*, which are data-gathering tools where the research participant makes notes or responds to quick questions throughout the time period under investigation. Sometimes this looks like a person keeping a log or journal for a day or several days of what they are doing with their time, with open-ended questions about elements a designer may ask them to pay attention to (e.g., note what time you ate, and where you went to get food in the building, and who you ate with). Sometimes this looks like a set of mini-surveys, either on paper or digitally, that ask participants closed-ended questions about what they were doing for the last hour or so. In either case, participants are also often asked whether what they have been doing is typical or atypical for the time of day or day of the week they're recording data. The data from this method is more likely to yield accurate portrayals of how people actually spend their time. After all, if I asked you what you were doing and where you were on the first Wednesday of last month between 9 and 11 a.m., how confident would you be in your ability to provide accurate and detailed information?

Timing and Pace in Data Collection: Before, During, and After the Design

In earlier chapters, I noted that it is important to consider the impact of gathering data from people who occupy or use designs all at once versus collecting data for one-at-a-time projects. On one hand, with smaller projects where the sample size is one or a few people, it is hard to generalize about a larger pattern about designs for any given designer or architect. It requires collecting these voices over time to make claims about how any particular designer's vision is made successful in the eyes of those who inhabit the designs. But even for projects where a big group of people offer their input, examining their ideas before, during, and after a design is implemented is crucial. We also need to think about how much time different methods with different sample sizes take to gather data. Doing a survey takes a lot of time and work on the front-end to design the survey questions, but the data gathering is quick and can include a large sample. Doing in-depth interviews, either with groups or with individuals, has smaller sample sizes but requires a lot of time to schedule, transcribe, and analyze.

So, given all of these temporal factors that impact the project, when is the right time to collect data from users, clients, and/or stakeholders in the design process to ensure you have helpful input before, during, and after a design is implemented?

Before the Design

Let's start with pre-design data gathering. As a client solidifies their desire to work with a particular architect or designer (or team), it is often based on whether early ideas that are shared can demonstrate that designers are taking user and client desires and needs into consideration. This means that before any design pen touches paper (in a physical or digital tablet), designers have already gathered data that will inform the design. This may occur in myriad ways, which can include instances when designers take informal notes in early meetings with clients to get preliminary ideas (e.g., jotting down client quotes such as "I want a brighter living space but I don't know how" or "I definitely want to avoid mid-century modern furniture in my waiting room because it may go out of style soon," etc.). It can also occur in more robust and systematic ways, such as when large architecture firms conduct focus group interviews with stakeholders about the needs they see for a future design. Regardless of how formal or systematic this pre-design data gathering looks, the most important thing to remember is to be intentional with the ways that input is sought.

During the Design

When I participated in meetings that were held to get feedback about the design of a college dining hall and residence hall, I paid particular attention to how the designs changed during the months of data gathering from various stakeholders. And I paid particular attention to how place mattered in the data. Case in point: before the design of a residence hall on the campus of my own employer, which is in Eastern Washington, architects had formulated designs that resembled more urban and "west-side" markers. In particular, this came across in color decisions. The colors of the rural location that were referenced by locals who commented in response to initial designs were: light blue like the sky, bright green like the spring wheat before it's harvested, beige like the wheat in autumn and dark brown like the fields in the winter as the snow melts. The designers had referenced more urban and forest-inspired colors, with dark greens, dark blues, and grays. It doesn't rain as much in Eastern Washington as it does west of the Cascade Mountain range, so the colors that invoked our sense of place needed to be adjusted. As a result of this mid-design deliberation, the fabric, paint, and lighting decisions were adjusted to reflect the stakeholders' sense of place. And now the residence hall that is buzzing with students is filled with light green chairs, light blue walls, and a sprinkle of golden beige. Gathering data during the design is crucial since iterative design yields a final project that captures people's input at every step. This is elaborated in the next section.

After the Design, with an Eye toward Future Designs

Post-occupancy evaluation (POE) is a common phrase in architectural and interior design research, referring to the assessment of buildings after they're built and after people start living in them and using them. Ever since the groundbreaking study by Van der Ryn and Silverstein of UC Berkeley residence halls, POEs aim to see if buildings are meeting the goals of the original design and to see if occupants are satisfied with the results (Hosey 2019). A lot of POEs have been one-time surveys, but there is a move toward more holistic and longitudinal analysis to see how designs may (or may not) work over time. POEs, though, are not used terribly often, in part because they can be expensive, in part because it can be risky to reveal problems with the design, and in part because it may seem a bit "too late" to change anything. But, as Bollo's (2021) feed-forward design framing helps us see, POEs can reveal how buildings perform over time and they can help designers and architects improve future designs, which make the whole design enterprise more sustainable.

Aligning Pre- and Post-Tests

Like many social science researchers, my data gathering, analysis, and write-up were disrupted by the COVID-19 pandemic. Between 2017 and 2019, I conducted a bunch of interviews, observations, surveys, and media analyses about second homes – those that people used for vacations with family members, and those that were rented out to others using short-term rental companies like VRBO and Airbnb. Enter the pandemic and all of the residential migration by urban folks to vacation homes that accompanied it in 2020, and my research trajectory with this data was not only delayed, but it was also threatened to be deemed outdated and useless. It was almost as if I had conducted pre-test interviews and surveys with people about their second home use, followed by a pandemic that has required me to consider whether a post-test round of data collection may be warranted (note to readers: this research is still in progress, and as of this writing I have edged closer to a more focused book project). Before, during, and after particular events, whether a pandemic or the completion of a large building or remodeling project, are key points to gather input from people whose lives are impacted by the spaces they occupy. In research projects aimed at identifying whether something has changed – either because a natural occurrence has caused a change or because the researcher (or designer) has implemented a change that they want to assess to see if it worked well – it is useful to conduct a pre- and post-test.

When Should You Analyze and Report the Results?

If you are conducting socially-informed research in the design process, you are going to be analyzing and reporting results throughout the project. At times the analysis is used within an internal group of people working on the design; at other times, it is collected and analyzed and shared formally with clients, users, or other stakeholders. In all cases, socially-informed research requires collecting data from people at multiple points in time and using the results from those data (which you have analyzed) to inform revisions along the way. It also requires that the people participating know that the designs are informed by their input, so presenting the results of your data analysis is a given.

Analysis of data is always ongoing in socially-informed research, and time to do the analysis should be considered when creating a project calendar. For example, if you are assessing a high school cafeteria redesign that included student survey data before the first draft of a design, you'd include time to design and distribute the survey and analyze the data. If you need to show the results of that survey data to high school administrators, contractors, or the school board, you'd also need to allow time to construct a presentation that visually represents the survey findings and is accessible to all members of the audience.

For many projects, the results of data analysis will be indirectly presented through the design. If users' input required the designers to rework a mock-up of a stairwell based on initial input from a beginning mock-up, the new mock-up will contain revisions based on the input. Users will see that. Design projects may also be informed by data analysis that occurred in past designs. This is part of the feed-forward design process (Bollo 2021) I discussed in Chapter 1. If you want to have your future designs be informed by current ones, then it is important to capture data that can be analyzed and organized into an accessible idea library.

Sharing or reporting your findings from socially-informed data collection includes varied audiences who make appearances at different temporal stages of the design. Beyond pre-design data collection, such as the survey of students before drafting ideas for a high school cafeteria, your design process will also include mid-design reporting to clients and users. This reporting may be more polished than the pre-project presentations of data seen only by the design team, but would likely be less polished than a design that occurs at the late stages before building. Of course, by that stage, most audiences are going to be interested in polished versions of the design itself. But it is also a good idea to present any data that supports the design in a beautiful way, too. Just as I described in the Introduction when I visited the Danish gallery exhibit of family life that included photography and data visualizations, the whole package of socially-informed design – including stakeholder input analyses – should showcase your attention to detail, your belief in creating socially-informed design, and your capacity to visualize ideas in understandable and beautiful ways. If your ultimate goal is to share the design and design process with academic or professional audiences, then taking time to visualize the results of your data collection (at all stages) is especially important. This is all elaborated in Chapter 5.

And one last tip that can save you time: as you set up your file management system, as discussed in Chapter 1, remember to include a navigable system to store all of the datasets, analyses, and visualizations of results at every stage of the design process. This will allow you to more easily learn from each project as you feed the ideas into future designs. In this sense, the organization and presentation of your data analysis may sometimes have an external audience, but it will always be there for you to use within your own design work. If you have stellar data analysis, visualization, and organization now, you will be better able to create a successful portfolio, and to tell the design story of large chunks of your career for any external audience in the future.

Time does indeed matter for socially-informed research in the design process. In explicit ways, there are discrete time periods and frequencies that are needed or recommended for whatever data collection and analysis you are using. But even in abstract ways, time matters for architecture and design. Even with a clear calendar and clear-cut tasks with predictable time needed to complete them, we all know that the design process may not happen in a linear way, and there are plenty of factors that can elongate the time needed for any part of a project. Design is iterative and non-linear. People who engage with the designs may change their minds about what they want during or after the design is completed. Plus, no design is fully sustainable as long as taste, resources, and cultural values change over time. But if designers and architects can embed systematic and careful attention to the role of time in the research process, then designs are more likely to be better informed by the voices of the people who will engage with them. Creating designs that people know they were part of creating will make those designs more sustainable. People are more likely to support the longevity and preservation of something that they believe they were part of.

Place and time seem like such obvious concepts for designers and architects to consider. In fact, this already happens in spades. Brilliant designs in our world that seem to be timeless and yet capture a historical moment are easy to find. Places that nurture universal human desires like comfort and calm can look different across varied cultural contexts, but they all speak to common human needs. We can also imagine designs that fail to capture elements of timelessness or universal human needs. More realistically, we know that design cannot be completely timeless or culturally or geographically universal. Change over time and across geographies is part of our social world. The built environment, while fixed in many ways, needs to be able to adapt to changes in our social world. Why not embed socially-informed research best practices such as the ones discussed in this chapter to allow for more adaptable and sustainable design? While considerations of form and function are part of every design, attention to data-gathering location, values concerning privacy, the amount of time it may take to design a short survey, and ensuring that data storage allows for easy access to inform future designs are just as important.

References

Bollo, Christina. 2021. "The Measure of Success." Paper presented at the American Institute of Architects National Housing Awards (online). May 3. https://network.aia.org/viewdocument/aia-national-housing-awards?CommunityKey=3934f0d4-c0c1-4600-b8a2-844131ba8365&tab=librarydocuments.
Hosey, Lance. 2019. "Going Beyond the Punchlist: Why Architects Should Embrace Post-Occupancy Evaluations." *Metropolis*, February 6. https://metropolismag.com/viewpoints/architecture-post-occupancy-evaluations/.
Janning, Michelle. 2008. "Public Spectacles of Private Spheres: An Introduction to the Special Issue 'Spaces and Places of Family Life: Cultural and Popular Cultural Representations of Homes and Families.'" *Journal of Family Issues* 29(4): 1–10.
Janning, Michelle. 2017. *The Stuff of Family Life: How Our Homes Reflect Our Lives*. Lanham, MD: Rowman and Littlefield.
Janning, Michelle. 2019. "Won't You Be My (Vacation) Neighbor? Second Homeowners and Changing Family Vacation Norms in the Sharing Economy." *Families as they Really Are @ The Society Pages* (August).

Telling the Data Story with Analysis and Presentation – Continuing the HOW

5

As someone who teaches about social scientific research methods every year, I occasionally attend conferences and take classes to brush up on my current skills and hopefully gain new ones. One such skill that I wanted to bolster was *data visualization* (or, as folks in the biz call it, "data viz"), which is a graphic and visual representation of data to make a data story accessible to a wide audience, even among those who do not have an understanding of statistical procedures. To this end, I went to a Tableau Conference a few years ago. Tableau (https://www.tableau.com/) is a data visualization program that is used in multiple industries to show and share complex (and sometimes not-so-complex) findings that may begin their life in a simple spreadsheet and end up in a flashy colorful interactive infographic that shows up on a website or publication.

The conference was great – constant activity, concurrent sessions showcasing all the bells and whistles of the latest version, vendors in a giant convention hall giving away their swag and shouting about the latest features of their products that were compatible with Tableau. I attended several sessions and began to realize, though, that I was sorely lacking in some basic data set management and statistical skills relative to the others who attended. I was also one of the oldest people there, or so I felt. I became so frustrated and insecure that I gave up learning about the program and instead began taking field notes on the behaviors of people attending. I pretended I was doing an "ethnography of data people," and drew maps, diagrams, and speech bubbles amidst the scribbled notes. I never did anything that resembles social science data analysis with these notes, as it wasn't any sort of formal research project. But I did look back at them recently, only to discover that I had created my

DOI: 10.4324/9781003183228-6

own doodled data visualization about the data visualization conference that was too complex for me to understand. My visual representations of my ethnographic data made sense to me, but I suspect any other audience who may want to understand my ethnography of behaviors of "data people" would prefer that I used a sophisticated program like Tableau to tell my data story. This story shows that not only do researcher skills matter in the analysis and presentation of data, but the audience matters, too.

How Do You "Find" the Best Findings? Returning to Ethics and Your Research Question

In Chapter 1, I discussed the importance of starting with a good research question. This cannot be stressed enough. Without a clear question, any data gathering will yield results that will not be useful. Nobody wants to participate in research if it is a waste of time.

But let's be realistic. Of course, research questions can change, especially if the research process is iterative. In fact, revised questions are a normal part of an iterative design process wherein designers may figure out that they're asking the wrong questions based on input from a previous question. For example, a design team may ask a family what kind of activities they envision happening in their redesigned living room. In the family's responses, it becomes clear that each person has a different set of desired activities. So, in the next iteration of the design phase, the design team would revise their question to "how can we design a living room that accommodates different kinds of activities?"

While questions may change throughout the design process, presumably the method to gather data to answer each question should lead to useful answers. So, if each segment of the design process is broken down into smaller data-gathering steps, each step should be done such that responses to research instruments will actually answer the question. In other words, regardless of whether it's an entire project or data-gathering steps within a larger project, the design of the data gathering should be informed by plans for data analysis. For example, while we cannot predict the future, we can design a survey of employees at a law firm so that our results can be presented in tabular form (that is, in a table) to clients, or we can design a neighborhood walk with interviews of residents near a location where a new hotel will be built so that our results can be presented with narrative and first-person quotations. In both of these cases, how we envision the data to be most helpful and to be shared with others informs the setup of the research instruments.

In most of my research projects, I inevitably have a moment where I wish I could go back in time to revise a survey or interview question. But I have to work with the data I have. I have to make the best of what I have designed. Any effort we make to get as close as possible to "no regrets" when we design a data collection procedure will put us in a better position to move forward with the design. This chapter, then, introduces data analytic steps and tools so that anyone designing a data-gathering process can have these potential outcomes in mind. So, while it's not exactly like finding treasure in a treasure hunt that we design, it comes close.

To start, I describe how a poorly-designed data collection process can yield bad analysis and bad results. After this, I discuss how a well-designed data collection process can still be ruined by a poorly-designed analysis. Both lead to the conclusion that thinking ahead to useful (and ethical) analysis should inform the design of the data-gathering steps.

Garbage in, garbage out. That's the saying in the tech world. Bad data collection practices yield bad analyses. It goes without saying that in socially-informed research in the design process, a primary goal should be to avoid garbage at any stage. This is true beginning with the research instrument (the survey or interview questions, for example). Asking people the wrong questions, asking the wrong people questions, or asking questions in a way that confuses people will all yield bad data. If you're interested in what activities are desired for a theater lobby, you wouldn't ask potential theater goers questions about their favorite colors (hmmm, these people prefer blue, so let's put a swimming pool in the lobby!). You also wouldn't ask people who would never spend time in this space the questions (hmmm, my mom likes cooking shows, so let's put a TV showing the Food Network in the lobby).

If "garbage in, garbage out" refers to how data that comes from a bad research instrument will be useless, then perhaps "treasure in, damaged treasure out" refers to inappropriate, misguided, or unethical analyses that don't capture the true story of well-constructed and helpful data. Bad analysis with good data can occur when we choose the wrong analytical tool to analyze our data, or when we misinterpret the data we have to tell a story that misses the true picture of people's experiences. Sometimes this is an ethical issue, as with cases of people's biases shaping their interpretation of data such that the answer they had in mind before they even asked the questions led them to their conclusions (rather than letting the data speak for itself). I have seen this take place when I advise student research. Sometimes students are so eager to prove an opinion they hold that they choose the wrong analytic technique (e.g., using only raw numbers to show group differences when a statistical significance test may show no significant group differences). Or they let their own views cloud their ability to notice patterns in interview data that contrast their views. Researchers are well-served to be prepared to find something unexpected, or maybe even undesirable. That's the way we learn – when we are surprised! And more importantly, we need to recognize that our preferences may guide a design, but they should not overshadow the patterns revealed in the preferences of users or residents. Since design should be iterative, decisions made along the way need to be made with careful and ethical interpretation of data. The next section details what these kinds of decisions look like in quantitative and qualitative data analysis.

How Do You Tell Stories with Numbers and Find Patterns in Stories? Understanding Quantitative and Qualitative Data Analytic Techniques

In my writing and speaking engagements (and in my teaching), I tell a lot of stories – stories about people I know, stories about people who've participated in my research, and stories about what I experience during research projects. Telling stories humanizes any research finding or social pattern. Even if I don't use people's real names, it is easier for people to picture the implications of my research findings if they can picture a real person experiencing it. In human-centered design, we sometimes use *personas* – fictional characters or created profiles that are composites of real data from people who may engage with a design in certain ways (Dam and Siang 2022). Think about some of the examples I've shared in previous chapters, such as the story about McKenna Vetter and her role as a brand new associate in a Las Vegas architecture firm, or the mother who told architect Romano Nickerson that a bathroom in a hospital design would not accommodate her son's needs. These stories bring to life design moments that a chart of numbers or aggregated data about the architecture profession cannot do. They also serve to showcase the importance of extreme cases, as was discussed in Chapter 3. Personas can do the same, except they are the composite stories of fictional people.

At the same time stories bring social patterns to life and highlight extreme cases that may alert designers to needed revisions, using only stories to make design decisions would not allow us to find important patterns in people's experiences. As I discussed in the Introduction, I note that research involves a systematic (scientific, really) method of posing a question that can be answered using quantitative or qualitative data, gathering and analyzing that data, presenting key findings as a way to answer the research question, and interpreting those findings using concepts and theories that come from fields that relate to the question. In this definition, stories would only play a role to highlight key findings gleaned from the systematically-collected and analyzed data. Or they could be included as a way to describe the experience of collecting the data (e.g., when presenting results of group interviews focusing on reactions to a proposed restaurant design, a designer could tell a story to the restaurant owner about how people were really excited to participate, or that they ate some delicious proposed menu items while participating in the interview). Finally, asking people to tell stories related to any factor you're trying to study can be part of a systematic data collection process that includes open-ended interview questions. The responses to the questions – the stories – thus become the texts upon which a systematic analysis can be conducted.

My take on all of this is that both stories and formal data collection, analysis, and presentation are good to have in any design process. But knowing when to use which one and in which combination is part of the process of data analysis (and setup of research instruments, actually). For big decisions that impact the design the most, systematic data wherein the researchers can feel confident that they've captured a clear and present pattern in attitudes or experiences is ideal.

Quantitative Data Analysis

Quantitative analysis of people's views or experiences usually stems from survey responses to closed-ended questions or observational data that involves counting instances of behaviors. In these analyses, researchers need to decide how sophisticated the analysis should be. It may be that saying something like "most of the people we talked with preferred X" suffices. Or it may be that more detail is helpful, such as saying "15 out of the 20 people we talked with preferred X." In both of these cases, presenting quantitative findings about a larger group can be useful in design phases where collective or shared views are needed beyond a few anecdotes or stories.

Once you have your data, there are important steps required before you analyze it. One step is called *data cleaning*, which is when a data set (usually quantitative, but can be qualitative) is put into a form where participants are de-identified (removing names, IP addresses, specific job titles, or other identifying information to keep people's responses confidential), where unnecessary metadata is removed (such as the timestamp of a survey), and where any variables that are included in text form (e.g., "yes" or "no") are recoded into numbers (yes = 1, no = 2) for any quantitative analyses that require statistical procedures beyond simply counting the number of each type of response.

Coding, by the way, is the process of turning the data as it comes to the researcher in raw form into data that is more manageable to organize, cluster, analyze numerically, and present in terms of patterns. This is discussed in more detail below in the section on qualitative analysis.

Recoding can also consist of merging or collapsing responses to closed-ended questions so that you have fewer types of answers. To illustrate this, if you ask what level of agreement people assign to the statement "I prefer minimalist design in my home," you may combine the people who select "strongly agree" and "agree" into one group, and do the same for those who select "disagree" and "strongly disagree." Sometimes recoding like this occurs because there are very few people in one of the (often extreme) categories. Having more people in each group can help with any statistical procedures. Sometimes recoding occurs because the researcher wants to give respondents lots of choices to capture their varying views, but doesn't really see much utility in distinguishing "strongly agree" and "agree" in the analysis phase because the main goal is simply to assess agreement. Of course, one of the drawbacks of merging or collapsing responses is the potential to underemphasize the variation in views among the people who participate in your research. It is important to strategize how much recoding and collapsing best answers the research question. If this can occur before data collection, great! But often decisions about this take place after data is collected, since only then do researchers know how many people may fit into any individual answer choice.

What kinds of statistical procedures are helpful when you have data that is quantified (or could be recoded in order to become quantified)? Presenting frequencies is common. So is presenting *measures of central tendency* (means, medians, or modes – the average, middle value, or most common response that show us how an overall sample looks "on average" or "for the most part"), which can provide a quick story about overall patterns in the data. Some people prefer that numeric data should be analyzed using more sophisticated procedures besides counting frequencies such as analysis of variance (ANOVA), chi-square tests, *t*-tests, correlational analyses, or regression, which are all different kinds of statistical procedures that allow for significance tests. These tests are used with data from more than one variable analyzed together and are chosen based on the level of measurement of the variables. As a reminder, level of measurement refers to the type of variable you're working with. If it is a variable where all of the answer choices are categories that cannot sensibly be ranked (e.g., favorite furniture style), it is called a categorical or nominal variable. If answer choices can be ranked but they're not necessarily numbers that have real mathematical meaning and may not have equal distances between them (e.g., the level – on a scale of 1 to 5 – that people like a particular furniture style), it is called an ordinal variable. If answer choices are actual numbers where calculating a mean makes sense (e.g., how many pieces of furniture from a particular style do people already have in their spaces), it is called an interval-ratio variable. It is important to think about what level of analysis you'd like to use as you envision your data analysis and presentation. If noting proportions of people who prefer different furniture styles suffices, use nominal variables. If noting how strongly people prefer certain styles, use ordinal. If noting actual numbers of furniture pieces, use interval-ratio.

While going into detail about each of the aforementioned statistical procedures does not occur here, naming them can at least point you to sources where you can explore more. These kinds of analyses require collecting data in a way that findings would not be a result of biased sampling or other factors that would make the data less objective. This level of quantitative analysis is needed if claims about group differences need to pass muster among audience members for whom scientific approaches are required. For example, if you counted the number of times a certain amusement park path was used by adults and children and wanted to see if the difference between the two age groups was a statistically significant difference, you'd use interval-ratio level data to measure path use (and nominal or ordinal data to measure age group), and you'd conduct statistical tests to assess actual differences between the groups (such as a t-test, which tells whether means for two groups are statistically significantly different, which means the difference reflects actual group differences rather than the differences resulting from chance).

Qualitative Data Analysis

Qualitative data is not focused on numbers or statistical significance, nor is it often meant to be able to generalize to a larger population, but it can be analyzed just as systematically as quantitative data. When a project is more about stories than numbers, qualitative data is particularly helpful. But even projects that require tables, charts, or other ways to show numeric patterns can come from qualitative data. I begin this section with how to find patterns in qualitative data that are more about themes than numbers, and then I transition to instruction on how to transform qualitative data into data that may be analyzed numerically.

If you've ever read a summary, analysis, or abridged version of a book or film, you have seen a type of qualitative analysis. In reading a short overview of a larger text, you decide whether to trust the author in their ability to capture the main themes, plot lines, tone, and characters. Usually, this trust comes from a reader finding a published author or critic to be a trustworthy source by virtue of the review being published in a reputable outlet (and it helps to agree with the summary or review in that process of establishing trustworthiness). When it comes to presenting qualitative findings in a sociological research study, however, trust is more likely to be established by the author's inclusion of rigorous and systematic methods used to "find" the themes and patterns in the text. In this sense, qualitative data can be analyzed scientifically.

How does this work? Qualitative researchers code the data. As mentioned above, coding is the process of turning the data as it comes to the researcher in raw form into data that is more manageable to organize, cluster, analyze numerically, and present in terms of patterns. Coding has also been defined as "how you define what the data you are analyzing are about" (Gibbs 2007: 2). As researchers analyze texts or notes or images, they identify and organize excerpts that seem to exemplify the same theme. Each theme identified is called a code. For example, if you conducted an interview study and asked people to "please discuss your favorite color" (in an open-ended question, not a question where you provide the answers), you may get responses such as "I love red," "Magenta is my favorite," "I prefer green," "I don't have a favorite color," "I like red and green equally," or "I'm color-blind so I don't know." In order to code this data, the answers can be clustered together into categories – or codes – that are more useful for analysis and presentation. For example, depending on the research, responses that show preference for red and magenta may be grouped together into a "prefer red/magenta" code. Green may be its own code. And the other three statements may be clustered together into an "other" code or may be singled out if it makes sense. "I like red and green equally," for example, may be coded into either or both of the red and green codes (noting that some people are included more than once in the presentation of findings). You may also decide that "I don't have a favorite color" and "I'm color-blind so I don't know" may fit together since they both refer to people whose opinions on color choice are not about actual colors. Just as with deciding how and whether to recode data, discussed earlier in the quantitative analysis section, coding requires careful decisions about how and why phrases and sentences (or other kinds of qualitative data) may cluster together. The deliberations about coding require a researcher to recall what the research question is, what variability within answers may be needed to make decisions, and how audiences may interpret the findings. So, if you have clients for whom magenta and red are starkly different colors, then clustering them together in your coding process would not work well.

How does coding work? How do you decide what themes emerge from a qualitative data set such as interview transcripts or field notes of observations? While there are hundreds of different terms and approaches to qualitative coding in the social sciences, here I present three approaches that are likely to work well in design projects: the descriptive/analytic method, the open/axial/selective method, and empathy maps. These can be combined and many elements of each overlap, but it is most helpful if they are described separately.

Descriptive/Analytic Coding

The *descriptive/analytic method of qualitative data coding*, referred to by Graham Gibbs in the 2007 book *Analyzing Qualitative Data* as thematic coding and categorizing, asks researchers to think about how qualitative data can be examined as surface-level descriptions and under-the-surface themes with meaning that can only be discovered by coding through several rounds. A *coding round* is a step where the researcher carefully examines all of the text being analyzed, noting patterns, and building off of previous rounds. Subsequent rounds offer new codes, added depth, and connections between codes. Usually, qualitative researchers go through at least two or three rounds of coding. The rounds of coding often begin with descriptive codes. In the example about favorite color, the descriptive codes may be "reds," "greens," and "other." These are, in a sense, the nouns that describe in a fairly straightforward way what types of answers emerge in the data. These codes are often words that are the same as respondents' words. This kind of coding can be likened to a word cloud, where the coding round yields the words and their frequency of use in participants' responses. This is helpful but is often not enough.

In order to understand the meaning behind the responses, it is useful to move toward categorization: codes that capture features that the first round of descriptive codes may have in common. For the favorite color data, it is possible to imagine categorization wherein the full set of responses are categorized into two codes: "prefer particular color(s)" and "do not discuss particular color(s)." After this kind of categorization, a researcher usually starts to wonder what these kinds of categories mean. Sometimes this involves creating sub-codes (or "child codes," as if the first rounds of coding of big categories are the "parent codes").

If people are asked "please discuss your favorite color" and the categorization reveals interesting themes in the "do not discuss particular color(s)" code, it is useful to look more deeply by using analytic codes: themes or patterns that are implied or noticeable after the researcher places excerpts into codes that tell a deeper story than may be seen on the surface. For the favorite color data, look closely at the "I" statements where no color is discussed: "I don't have a favorite color" and "I'm color-blind so I don't know." In the analytic stage, a researcher can move beyond the "do not discuss particular color(s)" code and posit certain bigger themes such as "when color is not the central design question that should be asked," or even "does asking about color signal that visually-impaired individuals are excluded from the design process?" For an astute designer gathering qualitative data from end users, clients, or other stakeholders, it is important to go beyond description and categorization. Analytic coding can offer bigger picture interpretation of context (including cultural contexts in which choosing a favorite color may be less important than other elements of design), meaning, and experiences that may be more hidden than obvious answers to a question about favorite color (Gibbs 2007). In addition, moving into analytic coding ensures that the design and research process are iterative. It is common for qualitative researchers to see things differently as they code the data and uncover deeper patterns and meanings that descriptive coding on its own offers. This means that reflective qualitative coding is often reflexive – likely to point to areas where our own biases and views shape and are shaped by the data.

Open/Axial/Selective Coding

The *open/axial/selective coding method* offers researchers a clear and rigorous set of tools to understand patterns and meaning in qualitative data (Williams and Moser 2019), and the steps involved map well onto the descriptive/analytic technique already discussed. The two techniques are very similar, yet offer different concepts and terms for each coding step. Often, qualitative analysis is *inductive* – letting the data lead to explanation for what is happening (and why), rather than *deductive* – starting with hypotheses or theories that dictate what codes and patterns should be used and tested within the data. Another way to think about inductive research is to imagine that the data develops the story and leads to its conclusion (with the researcher's help), rather than the story's presumed conclusion being used to test whether the data fits. In this way, analysis starts with open coding – a process whereby a researcher identifies categories and codes and themes that emerge from the data. Only after codes emerge from the data does the researcher classify or organize responses in the form of patterns. This is similar to the descriptive coding rounds discussed earlier.

After one or more rounds of open coding, the next stage is axial coding – looking at the emerging themes and codes and categorizing and aligning them. Just like categorization, axial coding includes clustering codes into groups that show their relationship to each other. Overlapping open codes turn into axial codes when they are grouped together based on some sensible similarity or relationship. This stage of coding can include various methods to ensure the emerging themes make sense. One method is the constant comparison method, wherein the researcher goes line-by-line in the data in an act of ongoing and iterative comparison of codes, new data, and emerging themes. This technique – often done in several coding rounds – ensures that the main themes are comprehensive and consistently present in the data.

Once axial coding is underway, the deepest level of coding – selective coding – takes place. Selective coding is more abstract than coding done in earlier stages. It is a movement away from counting and naming and toward specifying themes and explanations for patterns. In the favorite color question discussed earlier, selective coding is the stage that would lead the researcher to understand the deeper meaning behind seemingly benign answers to a question about favorite color, meanings that may include themes of context and access. For designers who may wish to keep track of themes that emerge from a career's worth of projects, this kind of method can lead to theory development for design more generally.

Empathy Maps

Descriptive/analytic and open/axial/selective coding techniques for qualitative data analysis are used in many fields, from sociology to medicine to business. The coding rounds that move from description to deeper meanings about context, access, and values are useful in design research as well. A third helpful technique – *empathy maps* – comes from the world of design thinking and user experience (UX) design research. Empathy maps are meant for researchers to understand the point of view of end users. Empathy maps are visualization tools that help researchers summarize and make sense of what users convey during design research and offer a way to articulate this to various audiences in order to meet users' needs (Dam and Siang 2021). The methods used to gather user data usually include verbal brainstorming sessions and can include surveys, group interviews, or even observational research during a site visit where participants explore features that are part of a design. The maps include four quadrants: says, does, thinks, and feels. These capture, respectively, what participants say in the form of direct quotes, what users do or show during the research process, what users think about any aspects of the design (usually gathered via good interview questions that allow for comfort and honesty), and what users' emotional responses are during the experience itself. Sometimes additional sections of "pains and gains" – user frustrations and goals – are included.

Empathy maps differ from the aforementioned techniques because they are used during both the data gathering and analysis phases of research (indeed, they could have easily been included in Chapter 2). The quadrants can be made visual to participants during the research wherein sticky notes with participant words, actions, thoughts, and emotions are placed in relevant quadrants. The analysis by those facilitating the empathy mapping consists of noting whether any quadrants are more or less populated than others, with an eye toward gathering more data if any quadrant looks empty. The next analysis steps mirror the earlier methods: cluster data together that looks similar (descriptive coding, open coding), name the clusters based on the main theme they convey (categorization, axial coding), and then work with fellow researchers to uncover repeated themes, gaps, and insights (analytic coding, selective coding).

In empathy mapping, the primary goal is to find ways to design something that meets the needs of end users whose views and experiences make up the data gathered. What participants say and do (and think and feel) informs the iterative design process. Needs that emerge from this process can be organized by starting with verbs and action words, along with traits of the users and any contradictions or inconsistencies (either across group members or between words and behaviors for one member). Then these data can be arranged using Maslow's hierarchy of needs based on his 1943 "A Theory of Human Motivation:" first fulfill basic physiological needs such as eating and sleeping, and then move to higher level needs such as safety, love, and self-actualization (Dam and Siang 2021). Returning to the inductive/deductive distinction, empathy maps offer a bit of both: the researchers don't necessarily know what may emerge from participants' words, thoughts, and behaviors, but they know they'll organize them into discrete quadrants (or initial codes) and eventually order them according to the type of need. Themes emerge from the data, but the initial sorting tools are figured out beforehand.

A final word about coding. My husband is also a sociologist and has conducted wonderful qualitative research about college student experiences (see Christopherson 2020). His research includes annual interviews of students across six years as they journeyed through the college experience and beyond. As he began his research and listened to the interview recordings, he found himself wanting to remember certain quotes just because they were interesting. He wasn't sure why, or what eventual code or theme they may fit into, but he had a feeling that some of the things students said would be good to preserve in one place. This place was his code entitled "Quality Quotes." Sometimes they were just funny quotes. Other times they were quotes that signaled larger social issues even if only one student was quoted. And a few were quotes that somehow captured the essence of the project in ways that other voices could not convey. Many of these quotes ended up in the final book. I use the same technique, often naming the code something along the lines of "cool quotes that we're not yet sure about but know they're good to note." I recommend doing the same in any coding process in design research. You never know when a quirky or insightful individual quote can capture an important collective reality or offer you inspiration.

Transforming Qualitative Data into Quantitative Data

Quantitative and qualitative data are fairly easy to differentiate – either the data is numeric or narrative. But it is common to transform qualitative data into quantitative data. By using the coding techniques described earlier, researchers can turn codes into numbers by counting how often certain codes occur in any given set of data. So, for example, if designers collect open-ended interview data about how to create a sense of comfort and welcome in a new hotel entrance from 20 local residents, they could count how many interviewees mention how much the artwork represents the history and culture of their neighborhood. If most interviewees note this as important, and if the individual interviewee is the unit of analysis, findings could be represented with a frequency or even a pie chart (e.g., 15 of 20 local residents [three quarters of a pie chart] discussed neighborhood historical and cultural representation in artwork as mattering in creating a sense of comfort and welcome).

I have done this kind of data transformation in my survey research on love letters. I asked respondents an open-ended question about where they stored their romantic communications. I coded the responses using the open/axial/selective method discussed earlier. In the first round I coded responses into digital (e.g., computer folder) or physical (e.g., nightstand) locations. I created sub-codes for each and then focused primarily on physical locations. I noticed that most respondents used prepositional phrases to describe the physical storage locations (e.g., under the bed). In the axial coding round, I coded the physical location prepositional phrases as fitting into either "in, under, behind," or "on," indicating the level of visibility and accessibility of the love letters. In the selective coding round, I divided the sample into men and women and counted the proportion of location codes for each, finding (using statistical procedures that allowed me to say whether groups were statistically significantly different) that women were more likely to store love letters "in, under, and behind" things and men were more likely to store them "on" things. In the selective coding round, I also figured out explanations for why men would place love letters on a dresser and women would place them in a drawer. Ultimately I concluded that women are more likely than men to feel responsible for maintaining family kinship keeping and household tidiness, thus leading to a greater numeric proportion of women storing love letters in less visible (and thus better preserved) places than men. I went from coding open-ended data using an inductive approach to presenting numeric gender differences using statistical significance tests (Janning and Christopherson 2015).

In earlier chapters, I discussed how a set of data may be compiled all at once (as with a survey used in one design project), or may be collected over time (as with interviews of clients one at a time over several months). In both cases, the data can be analyzed and shared to inform ongoing design, or to show potential clients the outcomes of past designs.

Data can also be divided into sub-groups within any sample, just as I did with my love letters research. All data has the potential to be sorted into groups based on whatever is interesting to the researcher. Even in one survey or interview, everyone can be asked the same questions and then the researcher can divide the answers into salient groups and compare them. This can be done with qualitative or quantitative data, or it can be done where researchers transform qualitative data into quantitative data, as I described happening in my own research. Analyzing data within different stakeholder groups can be really helpful for any designer who wishes to see how group membership and status may impact responses to questions about a design. It is rare to have everyone agree about a design, even in a small group such as a family. Setting up data collection to be able to analyze data across groups is important. Using particular tools to allow for easy data analysis, including separation by group, is helpful, which is the subject of the next section.

How Do You Know Which Analytic Tool to Use in the Marketplace? Digital and Paper Notebooks, Spreadsheets, and Qualitative Analysis Programs

This section focuses on what data analysis actually looks like in terms of work, where the work takes place, and what tools are used to end up with useful results – what Gibbs (2007) calls "the mechanics" of coding. I have used all of the tools described in this section, sometimes choosing a tool based on availability (e.g., some technology was not available ten years ago, some tools have been funded at my institution and some have not). Ideally, we use tools that best analyze the data we have. But realistically, it is helpful to know how to work with what we have. Below I describe tools that are commonly used to organize, sort, and analyze data to be used to inform design for clients and stakeholders (and sometimes used to make claims to wider audiences via formal research dissemination and communication channels). I start with physical tools and then move to digital tools, naming a few products in case readers would like to try them out.

Pen-and-Paper Analysis

Pen-and-paper coding works well once you have documents that you can physically touch, spread out on a surface, and write or draw on. Most of what I discuss here refers to textual data, like open-ended survey responses or interview transcripts. But it can also be applied to observational field notes, maps, drawings, or even images. Imagine a stack of printed interview transcripts from the 20 people interviewed about the hotel lobby discussed above. In an open coding round, as codes are developed, they are noted in the margins of the papers. Often, different codes are assigned different colors. Alongside text portions that belong in a certain code is a vertical line representing that code by color. If the margins are wide, which is a good idea, multiple codes can apply to the same text excerpt. In pen-and-paper coding, researchers can also circle keywords, draw arrows between coded text, add notes or memos in the margins, and use highlighters to emphasize themes that may connect codes.

In empathy mapping, the pen-and-paper coding can occur simply by putting the sticky notes in quadrants on a vertical board in the room where people are participating. While no colors or pens demarcate the codes, and while it is harder to put a sticky note into multiple quadrants than can occur in pen-and-paper coding, the physical organization of sticky notes that are in the same group fulfills the same function as pen-and-paper coding. This type of coding is simply a physical visual grouping of data into codes without using a computer program to sort.

For these physical coding processes, being able to retrieve text from the codes is important to plan before gathering data. In either pen-and-paper margin coding or empathy mapping using sticky notes on a board, researchers can take a look at their coded data and make note of any number of things, including the proportion of text that is coded using a certain color, or even the number of topics shown in text excerpts that are coded into multiple codes (which is often referred to as *code co-occurrence*). These require the ability to see all of the text excerpts in each code. This is why having space to spread out the printed documents is particularly helpful. Ultimately, you want to be able to retrieve all of the text that falls under each code, put that text in one place (noting which participant it came from by number, name, or pseudonym), and read through the excerpts to get the complete "story" of that code. Doing this also helps researchers figure out if they need to add sub-codes, especially if the story of one code reveals that there are very different types of responses that can be grouped together within that code. As you can imagine, this coding method requires a lot of paper, photocopying, colorful pens, movement of text chunks from one place to another, and/or sticky notes that can be easily moved and clustered (Gibbs 2007). Coding itself requires not only props but also an active choreography that allows the codes to be visible, sortable, and changeable.

Digital Data Analysis

There seems to be a new digital tool that can be used to analyze data introduced every year. Just when I think I have a handle on one statistics program, a new one comes out that costs less (but that may require a year of training just to understand how it functions). When it comes to quantitative data, which often comes from survey research (but can also stem from counts of space use, people, or amounts of time people spend doing certain tasks in certain spaces), there are numerous tools that can be useful. Some require familiarity with particular platforms that are fairly common and accessible even for home computer use (e.g., Microsoft Excel or Google Sheets), while others require a hefty fee or organizational subscription. And some may be financially accessible (as some open-source statistical programs are) but require a steep learning curve. I describe a few digital data analysis tools here and note what kinds of projects may be best suited for each.

I am a fan of spreadsheets for quantitative data management and analysis, and I oscillate between Microsoft Excel and Google Sheets, depending on which computer I'm using and whether I have internet access. Excel and Sheets are tabular spreadsheet programs that allow users to populate rows and columns with data. In these programs, the rows are usually people who participate in my research, and the columns are the variables included in the study. Each person's responses to each question are shown in the cells in their row (a cell is one of the small boxes in the spreadsheet). Without going into detail about how this works (there are countless online tutorials for these kinds of spreadsheet programs), suffice it to say that any patterns in the data can be seen by sorting, summing, or calculating within the programs themselves. This means you could have a spreadsheet with 800 rows (each a person) and 5 columns (each a variable), plug in some instructions, and end up with a table showing how many people scored each "score" on each variable. While the raw data is a 5 × 800 spreadsheet, it can be simplified into digestible and visually-appealing tables showing clusters of responses instead of individual responses.

If you create surveys to collect data, such as Google forms or Qualtrics or Surveymonkey, likely you have seen spreadsheets showing the data that these programs produce. These are particularly useful if your analysis is relatively simple and straightforward (count people who chose each answer for each question you asked). But if you want to look at relationships between variables (perhaps by separating answers on one question into demographic groups, or by creating cross-tabulations that show where each respondent lies in their responses to two questions), or collapse responses into bigger categories (as discussed earlier), then Qualtrics is really the most useful tool. Most online survey programs allow you to export the data into a spreadsheet program such as Excel (or as a.csv file), which you can use for more sophisticated analysis and table creation. Most of these programs also create reports showing responses for each question asked, often in the form of bar or pie charts. In Qualtrics, for example, you can edit these to be a certain color, show percentages or raw numbers, or change the title or axes, and then export the data visualization into a report or presentation. This program allows for more complexity and capacity to run some statistics and divide groups a bit more clearly than the other programs.

For statistical analysis meant to generalize to a population or to share in an academic setting, and for those who are familiar with techniques of inferential statistics, then using a statistics program such as Stata, SPSS, R (open source), or Jamovi (open source) will be helpful. As with Excel and Qualtrics, doing online tutorials can be a really helpful way to get to know these programs' capacities. For those people on the "keep things simple" end of the spectrum, knowing how to at least enter and use data in a computer spreadsheet such as Google Sheets is a great skill to hone.

Numbers aren't the only data that can be analyzed using a digital tool. Qualitative data analysis software has come a long way since the late 1990s when I used it for my dissertation research. In addition to software that can transcribe audio files (albeit not terribly accurately), there are digital tools that mimic the pen-and-paper coding techniques described above. Most simply, using a word processing program such as Microsoft Word or Google Docs can be used to create color codes for text excerpts, either by changing the color of the font or by adding highlighted shading. It's a bit harder to code any single excerpt with more than one code, though, since any word or space in the document can only be made into one color at a time. These word processing tools are useful for coding when the analysis is simple or has very few rounds of coding. Otherwise, you'll want to create separate documents for each code, where you copy and paste text excerpts (and respondent ID #s) into each document.

Because word processing programs can be cumbersome for coding, it can be really helpful to get familiar with programs designed to allow for more streamlined qualitative analysis (and not word processing). NVivo and Dedoose are the two I've used, though there are others in the marketplace, including Atlas.TI and MAXQDA. Even Qualtrics can take open-ended survey responses and create word clouds or look for frequencies of certain words or phrases (which technically counts as coding, but doesn't offer the same depth and richness as the coding techniques I described earlier).

NVivo and Dedoose are particularly useful if you have numerous files to analyze. Let's say you have 20 interview transcripts, each 8–10 pages long. That's a lot of paper to print for pen-and-paper coding! Using a qualitative data analysis program allows you to very quickly highlight text from any file, put it into a code that you create, and then move through the rest of each file doing the same. You can code excerpts into multiple codes, create sub-codes as you go, add memos to your codes, check for code co-occurrence, and – most importantly – know automatically which person the excerpt belongs to (because these programs automatically note this as you code). Thus, reading the "story" of any given code is as easy as going to that code, reading all the excerpts (that you put there), and knowing which people (and how many) said the things included therein. These programs vary in price, with NVivo requiring a bit more expense and a download to a hard drive, and Dedoose offering a modest monthly subscription that allows for use by more than one researcher at the same time. These programs are particularly helpful if you envision your findings needing to be shared with an academic audience, or if clients (or you) require being able to save time and show systematic coding that can be shared digitally and transformed quickly into data visualizations.

How Do You Tell Your Future Self the Data Story So the Next Design Will Be Better?

This chapter has been devoted to how to tell your data story, but who is the audience for this story? The audience always includes yourself, since feedforward design (Bollo 2021) incorporates what you've learned from past design into the present and future design. Data analysis is essentially presenting "what you've learned" systematically and clearly so that patterns revealed in a design process can help future designs be better. But just because you may be your first audience for your data analysis doesn't mean the analysis and presentation of data should be any less rigorous or careful. Our memories are flawed, so following the aforementioned steps for quantitative and qualitative data analysis even for work that will only be seen by your eyes will help you know what worked and what didn't. This is helpful for projects where data collection informs steps within one project, and for projects where data collection (often after the design is completed) can inform future projects.

While carefully telling the data story is useful for individual designers, in many cases, designers work in teams. Thus, participating in careful data analysis and presentation will help anyone continue work on a project or work on future projects that are informed by a current project. This means that putting your findings into an accessible format for other audiences will be helpful. Sometimes this also means presenting findings in visually-appealing forms to business stakeholders so that future projects may be justified or used in marketing materials.

Perhaps the most important audience members for data presentation are the clients and end users themselves. As the design process unfolds, at each step designers ought to present findings from the previous step as an explicit justification for design decisions. So, if an architecture and design team conduct focus groups with college staff and students about preliminary designs for a new residence hall, the carefully figured findings from those focus groups should be discussed as introductory material in the next design iteration. This is socially-informed research not just because the people who will be engaging with a design have had their voices included in the design process, but because the designers explicitly talk about the inclusion of these findings as they propose their design. This is a case not just of doing the research, but talking about the research outcomes with those who participated in it.

For data analysis where the end result is formal presentation of data in outlets such as peer-reviewed journal articles, exhibits, or conference presentations, the audiences are likely to be other design and architecture professionals. Necessarily, data analysis in these cases must adhere to professional standards that may include getting approval from an Institutional Review Board (as with university-sponsored research), data presentation using particular tabular or other visual style guidelines, and notes about formal research procedures. In these cases, the presentation of findings often follows a formal methods section, where the authors of the research discuss sampling procedures, limitations, data instruments (such as surveys and interviews), variable operationalization, justification for qualitative or quantitative analysis, and formal data analytic procedures and tools.

There are thus two types of external audiences who require aesthetically pleasing and formalized data analysis presented in visual forms: end users or clients and other design and architecture professionals. In both cases, data visualization and presentation of findings are worthy of discussion, which is the focus of the next section.

How Do You Tell a Well-Designed Data Story? Data Visualization, Presentation Tips, and Audiences

I always tell students when they are preparing to share their research at a professional conference to focus on no more than three key findings for their audiences. In part, this is because it's hard for people listening to a research presentation to remember more than that. It's also because the findings are easy for people to remember if for some reason any technology fails and visual representations are inaccessible. But really, narrowing key findings to only a handful is also a useful tool to help students focus on what they see as the big important takeaways of their work. This is useful for any researcher, regardless of whether you're presenting your findings to others or just to your future self. Selecting which data to present is not just a matter of sharing your findings with others, it is an exercise in selecting the data to tell the story that best informs your design.

In this book, you may have noticed that I do not have a lot of visual diagrams or tables. This is not because of my stunted Tableau skills. Rather, it is because the goal of this book is to help you understand the depth and context of socially-informed research in the design process (even though arguably some of what I present is a bit general). I believe you need words and paragraphs (and occasional stories) to get this kind of depth and context. But I understand the ways in which abbreviated or graphic representation of ideas can be helpful, especially for people learning new concepts. Thus, in the Conclusion, I offer a bulleted list of key ideas from each chapter so that readers can mark the concepts that matter to them, or that they may wish to study further.

In the meantime, I describe ways to share research findings with various audiences in order to make them accessible, organized, and designed well. I don't go into great detail about specific programs and features, because different researchers have different tools and skill sets. Instead, I discuss the basics of what each type of data presentation may look like and offer tips for best practices and pitfalls to avoid. Data visualization is not only used across many fields to show and share research findings, it is itself an interdisciplinary field of study dedicated to the graphic representation of mostly quantitative data (complete with conferences and countless credentials from data viz companies such as Tableau). Here I share ideas that are about the presentation of data more generally, which may or may not include graphic representations of quantitative data.

If you do have quantitative data, your presentation of research findings will include numbers, but these may or may not be represented with numerals. For example, let's say you are observing behaviors at two art gallery entrances. You observe 30 people in a 15-minute time frame. You may show the number of people who used one entrance or another in a mock-up of the gallery by using percentages (67% used the east entrance, and 33% used the west entrance), or by using pictures to represent proportions (twenty tiny people on the east and ten on the west). Depending on your tool and skill set, your analysis may be as simple as calculating frequencies such as these, or it may be as complex as figuring statistical significance when examining group differences (useful when you are analyzing the impacts of one variable upon others, not just for counts of people along one measure). Regardless of your stats prowess, keep the presentation of quantitative data at a level that people who have not taken statistics (or even pre-algebra) can understand and use. This is especially important in design projects where your goal is not professional publication, but rather the use of good data to make iterative design decisions.

Whether you are showing slides of numeric data that you made in PowerPoint or handouts you made in a graphics program such as Canva, or even if you are merely talking about numbers without any visual aids, keep those numbers simple. Share no more than a few numbers (or images that signify numbers) on any given slide or handout page. Choose the numbers that you think represent the big takeaways from the findings, perhaps even showing those numbers in bigger font than other items on any slide or page. But in choosing to present quantitative data in this simple way, keep in mind that you are also the one selecting which data to show. Numbers are powerful, and your role as a reflexive researcher who takes into consideration your own biases has to lead you to a careful and collaborative decision-making process about which numbers to show and highlight. After all, showing a slide with the number 67% in 76-point font will make audience members think that 67% is an important number. Think about whether this is the best number to show, whom it represents, and why you want people to remember it as they use data to inform their views throughout the design process. If your goal as a designer is to have equal numbers of people using the east and west entrances of a gallery, then showing a number that indicates you did not meet this goal may signify to an audience that you aim to remedy this.

For qualitative data, visualization and presentation strategies are less about numbers and more about stories. Recall that earlier in this chapter I suggested creating a code for any qualitative interview or survey data for really juicy or funny or interesting quotes. While it would be unlikely to use quotes in data presentation just because they're funny, you do need to think about strategic ways to incorporate quotes that are representative of ideas that are found as patterns in the data. Finding a powerful quote to signify a larger pattern for an entire sample of people whose words make up a qualitative data set is easy if you have followed the coding processes described earlier.

When you present qualitative findings in general, I recommend sticking with only a few key takeaways. Whether you represent patterns in the data that your codes reveal using images or words, be careful and strategic about what themes you are seeing and what impact sharing those themes will have on people's input in the design process. Be explicit about whether themes were present among a lot of people in the sample, or only among a few. If you choose to share findings that represent only a few people's ideas, talk about why you are doing this. For example, let's suppose that a majority of people who were interviewed in a project where architects and designers were reimagining a church to become a preschool noted that tearing down all of the interior walls was a good idea. Let's also suppose that (a) you have some great quotes that capture this sentiment ("tear down those walls!") and (b) most people who were interviewed were not child care professionals. Of course, excluding child care professionals from any data gathering about a redesign of a church into a preschool is a problem. But perhaps there were not many of these individuals available. Perhaps the largest sample of participants was avid churchgoers and people whose children were adults. In this case, a less common sentiment may be to keep walls, and perhaps even reinforce and soundproof them, so that there are quiet and private spaces for children who may have special needs (and who likely need naps). This sentiment comes from an important but numerically small constituency in the design – those whose everyday work and expertise give them a leg up in being informed about the design's needs. All of this is to say that, when presenting key findings from qualitative data that may inform iterations of a design, including themes that are substantively large even if they are not numerically large is a great idea. This, of course, speaks to the value of universal design, where the needs of one person, when met, would meet the needs of the entire community of people engaging with that design.

Most of this chapter has been about analyzing and sharing data within the group of people who are participating in the iterative design process. But, as someone who writes, speaks, and shares ideas frequently in popular media outlets, I would also encourage you to frame your findings in such a way that you could share your design story beyond the immediate project and beyond your own profession. The more design projects and their accompanying research are socially-informed, the better able architects and designers will be at contributing to the national dialogue about building sustainable communities. This contribution to our collective story is itself a demonstration of being socially-informed in the research and design processes.

References

Bollo, Christina. 2021. "The Measure of Success." Paper presented at the American Institute of Architects National Housing Awards (online). May 3. https://network.aia.org/viewdocument/aia-national-housing-awards?CommunityKey=3934f0d4-c0c1-4600-b8a2-844131ba8365&tab=librarydocuments.

Christopherson, Neal. 2020. *Transformative Experiences in College: Connections and Community.* Lanham, MD: Lexington Books.

Dam, Rikke Friis, and Teo Yu Siang. 2021. "Empathy Map - Why and How to Use It." Interaction Design Foundation. https://www.interaction-design.org/literature/article/empathy-map-why-and-how-to-use-it?gclid=Cj0KCQjwhLKUBhDiARIsAMaTLnHnGyjBvx2biTIDjDGERhW0BHcNwt0M4jIrNs57S5-8F1aFz3Z5418aAoLYEALw_wcB.

Dam, Rikke Friis, and Teo Yu Siang. 2022. "Personas - A Simple Introduction." Interaction Design Foundation. https://www.interaction-design.org/literature/article/personas-why-and-how-you-should-use-them.

Gibbs, Graham R. 2007. *Analyzing Qualitative Data.* Thousand Oaks, CA: Sage.

Janning, Michelle, and Neal Christopherson. 2015. "Love Letters Lost? Gender and the Preservation of Digital and Paper Communication from Romantic Relationships." Pp. 245–266 in *Family Communication in an Age of Digital and Social Media*, edited by Carol J. Bruess. New York: Peter Lang International.

Williams, Michael, and Tami Moser. 2019. "The Art of Coding and Thematic Exploration in Qualitative Research." *International Management Review* 15(1): 45–55.

Conclusion
Informing Future Design and Designing Socially Sustainable Communities – Revisiting the WHY

No offense to my social science colleagues, but there is nothing more satisfying for a sociologist who also loves design than talking with design professionals and getting lost amidst dizzying displays of furniture, lighting, flooring, and tech displays at a giant design conference. I recently attended the 2022 Hospitality Design Conference in Las Vegas, and I sought conversations where I could assess how much socially-informed design mattered to people in this industry. I displayed my name badge, clearly labeled "educator" (thus showing that I did not own a business or have resources to actually contract with designers), yet vendors still rushed to scan my badge and ask me about what products I needed for my hotel, restaurant, wellness center, or other hospitality business. These types of businesses are great locations to look at how socially-informed design may operate, in part because their business models are predicated on meeting needs of users over and above anything else. But the behind-the-scenes social parts matter, too, which I saw as I meandered through the displays and attended panel sessions. While some vendor conversations yielded helpful comments about their dedication to fair wages in developing countries where their products were manufactured, COVID-19 protections for workers, and environmental sustainability, I hit the jackpot when I found sessions with words like "democratic design" and "community" in the titles.

The "Making Design More Democratic" session included tips on how to use the design process to spread the ownership of design around, including to the people who will be using the design on a daily basis. This session included ideas from Victor Body-Lawson, founder and principal architect of Body-Lawson Associates Architects and Planners. Body-Lawson shared ideas about how architects and designers can create spaces that are infused with technology that would allow users to manipulate their own environments, from temperature control to colored lighting. Part of the iterative design process includes not only teaching end-users not only how to engage with the digital and physical elements of the design but also about new materials and systems that may even offer them transferable skills in the job market. The design process, thus, has pedagogical purposes. For example, if a building is built using local materials and people who live there are involved in the building process, they can learn how to use these materials for continued building projects. This kind of interaction between designers/architects, workers, and local communities is meant to give people autonomy and efficacy over their environments. Being socially-informed in this sense, then includes decentralizing some of the materials and labor so that local communities would not only benefit from an immediate design implementation but also may learn skills that inform future community development through design. With rapid spread of information across digital platforms (think YouTube videos for tile setting), architects and designers can create designs and systems that can be sustainable in various communities even after their design is built. Local sustainable design efforts not only reduce environmental impact, but they also reduce social inequalities, both within locales and globally. Add to this a democratization of design tools available online for much less money than even five years ago, and the designs become even more socially-informed.

In Chapter 3, I discussed the role of designer and architect expertise, which is crucial but must be balanced with the voices and experiences of those who are engaging with the design. In the same "Making Design More Democratic" session where Body-Lawson shared his ideas, interior designer and vice president of Determined by Design Sequoyah Hunter-Cuyjet called this "design equity." She noted that designers may favor particular styles, which are often wrapped up in their egos. This approach – style as ego – fails to account for the importance of people's stories. Including stories from end-users and other stakeholders is crucial for any equitable design, Hunter-Cuyjet says. In order for any design to work, it also has to be rooted in history, community, and neighborhood. It even requires going back to the indigenous history of a particular site and following the history across the varied social groups who occupied it. That historical and social context is a prerequisite to style and design. In addition, the contemporary stories, preferences, and even pop culture and fashion tastes of residents – often gathered through empathetic neighborhood walks and conversations – must be incorporated into the design. The tricky part of this is that, at times, stakeholders such as developers or owners are interested in design elements that may counter local residents' desires and experiences. Architects and designers practicing socially-informed research need to balance these sets of voices, never abandoning the goal of representing an authentic history and story of people who may reside there. And they need to do so with the social scientific rigor and high ethical standards I advise throughout the methodological steps outlined in this book.

Why Should You Keep Learning about Socially-Informed Design? Sustainability for Collaboration, Creativity, Career, and Community

COVID-19 brought with it a whole host of changes in how we use our living, learning, relaxing, working, and healing spaces. Architects and designers have taken note, citing an even greater need to listen to clients and end-users who desire convenience and flexible spaces that allow tasks and personnel to pivot. As I learned from designer Jou-Yie Chou from the design firm Post Company (in the "Designing with Soul" session at the 2022 HD conference), the monotony of quarantine has led to a desire for saturated immersive experiences, rather than an accumulation of stuff. In addition, the enhancement of the design process via digital tools such as virtual reality and AI (artificial intelligence) have offered new ways to offer clients immersive and realistic experiences before any building is built. Socially-informed research in the design process must account for what we have seen throughout the pandemic in order to meet people's changing social needs. Researchers must use new tools not just to showcase new designs, but to engage end-users and other stakeholders in ways that are inclusive and allow for their stories to unfold (even in virtual environments).

The HD session on "Holistic Wellbeing and Community by Design" was particularly fruitful for getting ideas that reflect changing needs for socially-informed research in design professions. This session was sponsored by the Hospitality Diversity Action Council, which – as noted in the HD conference program – is dedicated to "propel a more inclusive and equitable community," and to foster "open, honest conversations about diversity and equity challenges in the hospitality industry" (see https://hospitalitydesign.com/news/business-people/hospitality-diversity-action-council/ for more information). In this session, presenters noted the significance of the George Floyd murder and racial tensions in society as a catalyst for new approaches to design and architecture. Namely, they discussed how to engage a community deeply – really listening and providing resources for local residents (in the case of a non-residential design such as a hotel). This engagement may even include compensating participants for offering their voices and views in the research part of the design process, as presenter Damon Lawrence, co-founder of Homage Hospitality noted. Architects and designers need to invest time and resources in getting to know the people whose lives will be impacted by any design. People need to be brought into the design process, not just serve as beneficiaries of a completed building. This is more likely to lead to spaces that can adapt as a community changes and to spaces that are not superficial displays of cultural appropriation, because the community was looped into the design process as valuable stakeholders from the start. This can take more time and energy to do, but it's the right thing to do. As presenter Crystal Vinisse Thomas, Vice President and Global Brand Leader for Hyatt's Lifestyle and Luxury Brands, said, "we all want to drive revenue, but it'll be better if it works well." Having purpose leads to better design performance. And both require socially-informed research from the people who ultimately benefit from the design.

I have learned much from architects and designers who are already doing good work in socially-informed design. In many ways, the ideas presented here are simultaneously new and not-new. We all know that social issues matter in design. We also know that architects and designers have been paying attention to roles and relationships in society (and local contexts) for a long time. But it has become apparent to me that social sustainability as a priority in the work of designers and architects is still a relatively new idea, or at least is still mostly likely to occur among those designers who themselves have experienced social inequalities. All designers and architects can and should contribute to social sustainability in their work.

Recapping the Socially-Informed Research Steps from Chapters 1–5

This book is an attempt to collect and share the myriad good ideas about socially-informed research already present in design and architecture worlds, but to do so as a reframing and repackaging that includes some rigorous sociological insights along the way. In order to remind you of the key concepts and steps for socially-informed research in the design process covered in this book, I offer a recap of each of the key takeaways from the research steps discussed in Chapters 1–5, including some "big takeaways" for each chapter.

Before you read the list, though, perhaps a thought exercise may be useful. Think about a project you've worked on (or are working on) where you'd like to figure out whether it adheres to tenets of socially-informed design. Write down what you think are the key research questions asked in the project. Then, decide whether the research questions did help or would have helped you understand how well the design worked for the people inhabiting or using the design. Think about the types of questions each method discussed in this book helps us answer, and discern whether the method you used to gather input (if you used one) was helpful in answering your question. What were/would have been the benefits and drawbacks of this method? If you think more than one method could have been useful to triangulate your data, what second method would you have proposed, and why (and when, actually)? What did/would your sample and data collection procedures look like so that people could feel included and trust the process of data collection? How and with whom would/did you share findings along the way as you iterated design ideas? At what stages would ethics have mattered, and why? What larger cultural, historical, and community contexts mattered for this project, even if the people involved were localized? Do you think the design is actually working for people inhabiting it, and how would you know? After thinking through these questions, consider working through the checklist below to see if your research steps adhere to the goals of socially-informed design. In fact, I recommend going through this checklist for all of your projects.

Chapter 1: Framing a Project's Goals and Research Question – The WHAT

Defining the Type of Project and Data

- Understand and choose the right unit of analysis for your research; the entity (individual or group) being studied can affect the questions you ask and the findings you discover.
- Practice operationalizing (turning abstract concepts into measurable variables) so that your data actually answers your research question. Be sure any data gathered is meaningful, measurable, accessible, and trackable over time.
- Decide which level of measurement (categories, rankings, or numbers where a mean or other statistics can be calculated) is best for any variable included in your research.
- Plan research to include decisions about whether data collection will be cross-sectional (one moment in time) and/or longitudinal (data collected over time) and be able to explain why the choice best answers your research question.

Asking the Right Research Question

- When crafting a research question, consider community and other social needs in addition to individual or idiosyncratic needs.
- Decide whether your aim is to gather and analyze data to describe something or to explain why it is happening (and predict future impacts).
- Use your and others' past knowledge to craft a good research question that not only applies to an immediate project, but that can also connect to past and future design.

Setting Up Your Data Project

- Decide comparison benchmarks before you collect data. Benchmarks can come from comparing past outcomes with your current data, different group outcomes within your own data, or outcomes from your findings relative to an industry standard.
- Figure out (and design) as many of the nuts and bolts of your project as possible before the project starts. This includes attention to data storage, file naming and organization, and terminology.
- Build in ethics checkpoints at every stage of research, taking into consideration managing your biases, ensuring participant confidentiality and compensation, informing participants about how data will be used and shared, and representing findings accurately and carefully. Study Chapters 2–5 for further details about the importance of ethical decisions at every research stage.

Big Takeaways from Chapter 1

- When gathering data used to inform design, be sure to see larger patterns that any research design may yield, but don't forget the importance of individual stories – especially if they call attention to design features that align with universal design.
- Trust your expertise as an architect or designer at the same time you include the voices and experiences of those who will engage with your design. Informing future design should consist of a balance between expertise in terms of aesthetic choices and technical knowledge and people's use and views of the space. An over-reliance on either can result in good design that is never used (which arguably is not good design) or spaces that don't adhere to high standards in design.
- Practice architecture scholar Christina Bollo's (2021) "feed-forward design," building in enough iterative feedback and data-gathering steps to inform the final design, and use past designs to inform future designs.

A design portfolio is not a static collection of one-and-done designs; rather, it is an animated sequence of designs based on input from end-users, community members, and other stakeholders that inform each other and that create iterative improvements within and across projects and time. Set up all research projects in design with this as a goal. This creates more socially sustainable design in the future.

Chapter 2: Choosing a Research Method to Inform Design – The HOW

Stories and Numbers, Breadth and Depth, Reliability and Validity

- When you match a method to a question, know what each method offers. It also helps to think about whether quantitative or qualitative data (or both) would be helpful.
- When deciding what method to use to gather data (survey, individual interview, focus group, observation, or content analysis), consider how much depth or breadth you want, how efficient you need to be, and how much people's words or insights matter relative to observing their behaviors or studying documents or other "texts" that they may produce.
- As you decide how to operationalize variables, take into consideration both reliability (can be compared easily with past data) and validity (is actually measuring what you hope it measures).

Designing the Data Collection

- When crafting research instruments where you gather data from people, consider the impact of question ordering, accessibility of wording to the sample of people included (and err on the side of inclusivity), mutual exclusivity and exhaustiveness of possible answers to questions, and how it may be possible to use one research instrument for all groups of participants because answers can be divided by group in the analysis stage.
- Weigh the benefits and drawbacks of asking closed- and open-ended questions, both in terms of the data gathering itself and in terms of eventual analysis. When you think about what to ask people as you work on your designs, don't assume that open-ended questions will always get more accurate responses, and be sure that closed-ended questions include well-informed and complete sets of response options. For both survey and interview questions that are closed-ended, make sure your list of possible options is exhaustive, so that people who are interviewed will feel as if their answer is one of the ones offered.

- For any data gathering where the researcher is present, plan the "choreography" of the research itself, including seating arrangements, use of technology, use of recording and/or systematic note-taking techniques so that you don't have to rely on memory, and even eye contact.
- Decide the benefits and drawbacks of standardizing research instruments. More standardization allows for easier comparison across respondents, and less standardization allows for more elaboration from individual participants based on their idiosyncratic experiences.
- For focus group interviews and observation, it is helpful to have more than one researcher present to facilitate conversations (for focus groups) and notice things that others may miss while taking notes (for ethnographic observations).
- Decide how much you'd like the data-gathering process to be informed by design thinking, user experience research, and ideas from human-centered design.
- Decide whether triangulation will help in your research process.
- Always plan data analysis as you design research instruments.

Big Takeaways from Chapter 2

- Whatever method you choose should give you the right kind of evidence needed to move forward with a design. But the method you choose also must take into consideration the experience of users and stakeholders. In fact, in order to conduct socially-informed research in the design process, it is crucial to pay attention to the impacts on participants *during* the design process itself. If you do this, not only will the design be better able to meet the needs of users, it will also tell you something about the social context of the place being designed or redesigned.
- Collecting data is a social and sensory experience. Pay attention to the audio, tactile, and visual elements that are part of the research process, recognizing their influence and strategizing their use. A good test in the design process is to ask what senses will be invoked by users who occupy the space. Take a step back and also ask what senses should be involved in the process of seeking user input in the first place.
- The method used in data collection can make people feel more or less included and heard in the design process. Socially-informed design requires inclusion and plentiful opportunities for stakeholders to be heard, regardless of the formality and hierarchical structure of an organization.

Chapter 3: Choosing a Sample and Communicating with People during the Research Process – The WHO

Figuring Out a Sample

- When choosing whom to invite to participate in a research project (a sample), consider how representative potential participants are in terms of all of the relevant stakeholder groups who are impacted by the design.
- When choosing a sample, think ahead to data analysis and whether a probability or non-probability sample will work best to answer your question.
- Choose the most sophisticated sampling plan that is accessible and doable given your time, expertise, and resources.
- When deciding how many people in a sample constitute a good sample size in order for you to feel confident that your findings represent the overall population of interest, consider the types of data analysis that will be used in order to answer the research question. Deciding how many people to include in research is a matter of deciding whether breadth or depth is more useful to inform future design.

Communication

- Socially-informed design requires transparency. If people who are asked to offer input in the design process understand why they're being asked certain questions or placed in certain scenarios, they'll feel more comfortable participating. Implement informed consent whenever you ask people to share their insights to inform a design project.
- Don't underestimate the importance of clear, kind, and timely communications with all people involved in the research process in order to ensure that they feel included and valued.

Big Takeaways from Chapter 3

- Be a reflexive researcher by paying attention to the role of your (and others') bias and positionality. Make sure your research process is transparent to those who are invited to participate so that they know how their input will be used to inform the design. Part of that transparency is ensuring that participants know how you see your role in the process. Consider the impact of your status as either an insider or outsider to the group participating.

- Trust your expertise. Use it to inform the design along with the ideas of others. Expertise is not just about design but also about establishing trust and informing people about how their input will be used in the process.
- Empathize with people who participate in the research process that informs your design. This requires you to take into consideration the needs of all relevant social groups who may engage with the design.
- Status, power, and inequalities may affect who feels comfortable participating in research, how they may respond to the research process itself, and who controls their participation in the first place. A design will work better if it includes the ideas from those who otherwise may not have a chance to chime in. Implement strategies to create inclusive data-gathering processes, and think beyond the immediate stakeholders toward neighborhoods and communities when defining stakeholder groups. While people who are funding a project have a say in the design, a design will only work well if the varied experiences of all social groups are included.

Chapter 4: Setting and Pace for Data Collection – The WHERE and WHEN

Geographic Location, Types of Spaces/Significance of Place, and Privacy

- Cultural and geographic context, including any unequal access to resources within that context, affects the places where designs go. Recognize that wherever a design is placed, local customs, values, and ways of life must inform that design. It is every designer and architect's job to pay attention to that meaning for the people who occupy the spaces and for the communities surrounding them.
- Beyond practical or logistical variables, some decisions about where to work on the design are based on social and methodological factors that include access to users and users' behaviors, the establishment of trust between clients and designers, and even people's values concerning privacy and confidentiality.
- Accessing users is a key component of data gathering, and it is necessary to be present in a designed space (or existing space that needs to be redesigned) to observe and ask questions about people's use of the space. In most cases, this involves going to users, and not the other way around.
- The more public the setting, the less confidential people's views are and the less hidden the design project is from passersby. The more private the setting, the greater the likelihood that confidentiality will matter.

Timelines and Calendars, Pre- and Post-Tests, and Choosing Length of Time for Projects

- Before, during, and after particular events, whether a pandemic or the completion of a large building or remodeling project, are key points to gather input from people whose lives are impacted by the spaces they occupy. This multi-moment data collection process is necessary for iterative design.
- In research projects aimed at identifying whether something has changed, either because a natural occurrence has caused a change or because the researcher (or designer) has implemented a change that they want to assess to see if it worked well, it is useful to conduct a pre- and post-test.
- Designers and architects need to consider how much time they would spend (and how often) with people who will eventually be managing or using the space. How much people will be engaging with the design once built also affects timing and frequency of interaction. Timing matters in terms of planning a project, which includes thinking about what matters in pre- and post-tests, and setting up a realistic calendar.
- The designation of data collection as purely cross-sectional or longitudinal matters, but it matters less than the alignment of the data-gathering timing and technique with the design research question.
- In ethnographic observation, spend enough time so that people you're observing or interacting with "get real," wherein they lower their inhibitions and lessen moments of acting or pretending to come across as favorable.
- Figuring out how much time to spend gathering data from stakeholders in a design project requires a delicate balance: take enough time so people do not feel rushed, excluded due to low availability, or able to perform a role that may not represent what they're usually like but don't take so much time that project resources (and patience) are used up before a design is complete.
- Analysis of data is always ongoing in socially-informed research, and time to do the iterations of analysis should be considered when creating a project calendar.

Big Takeaways from Chapter 4

- Regardless of how formal or systematic this pre-design data gathering looks, the most important thing to remember is to be intentional with the ways that input is sought.
- Recognize that gathering data is, in itself, a social relationship between the researchers and the clients/users in a particular place and time. Designers

- asking people for their views should set up spaces and data-gathering techniques that allow for honesty and comfort. Designers should allow enough time for these techniques to be as inclusive as possible.
- Where you do your research matters. Going to the site of the design can establish trust. This occurs in both directions: users and clients trust you because you have made the effort and taken time to come to their space, thus building your capacity to empathize with their experience; and you trust the insights of users and clients because you are better able to understand the context in which they are making decisions and expressing opinions.
- Socially-informed research requires collecting data from people at multiple points in time and using the results from those data (which you have analyzed) to inform revisions along the way. It also requires that the people participating know that the designs are informed by their input, so presenting the results of your data analysis back to participants at each design step is important.
- Design is iterative and non-linear. People who engage with the designs may change their minds about what they want during or after the design is completed. Plus, no design is fully sustainable as long as taste, resources, and cultural values change over time. But if designers and architects can embed systematic and careful attention to the role of time, place, and other contextual elements in the research process, then designs are more likely to be better informed by the voices of the people who will engage with them. Creating designs that people know they were part of creating will make those designs more sustainable. People are more likely to support the longevity and preservation of something that they believe they were part of. Where and when the research takes place affects how much people feel that they're part of the design process.

Chapter 5: Telling the Data Story with Analysis and Presentation – Continuing the HOW

Returning to the Research Question, Method, and Project Setup

- Without a clear question, any data gathering will yield results that will not be useful. However, revised questions are a normal part of an iterative design process wherein designers may figure out that they're asking the wrong questions based on input from a previous question.

- While questions may change throughout the design process, presumably the method to gather data to answer each question should lead to useful answers. So, if each segment of the design process is broken down into smaller data-gathering steps, each step should be done such that responses to research instruments will actually answer the question.
- Asking people the wrong questions, asking the wrong people questions, or asking questions in a way that confuses people will all yield bad data. Bad analysis with good data can occur when we choose the wrong analytical tool to analyze our data, or when we misinterpret the data we have to tell a story that misses the true picture of people's experiences.
- Before coding or recoding any data, be sure to establish what steps you'll need to do for data cleaning. A tidy dataset makes for a more effective analysis.

Analytic Techniques and Tips

- Decide what types of statistical tests are useful for any quantitative data (or qualitative data that is transformed into quantitative data). This decision depends on researcher expertise, tools, and intended audience. For most clients and end-users, sophisticated statistical techniques are not needed. For peer-reviewed publication or presentation of data meant to be generalizable to broader projects or populations or if you want to make sound claims about group differences, however, it is helpful to learn and apply various statistical techniques when possible.
- When coding qualitative data using pen-and-paper or digital tools and techniques, be sure you go through enough coding rounds to reach clear patterns and themes that can be communicated to any intended audiences and/or transformed into categorical variables that can be used in quantitative presentation of data.
- In any coding project, create at least one code for quotes that strike you as important, intriguing, or even funny. You never know when they may be useful in your data story.
- For any coding processes (but especially important for pen-and-paper coding), being able to retrieve text from the codes is important to plan before gathering data.

Sharing and Presenting Findings

- Presenting quantitative findings about a larger group can be useful in design phases where collective or shared views are needed beyond a few anecdotes or stories.
- Focus on no more than three key findings in any data presentation.

- For data analysis where the end result is formal presentation of data in outlets such as peer-reviewed journal articles, exhibits, or conference presentations, the audiences are likely to be other design and architecture professionals. Necessarily, data analysis in these cases must adhere to professional ethical standards that may include getting approval from an Institutional Review Board (as with university-sponsored research). Professional standards about data presentation using particular tabular or other visual style guidelines, and notes about formal research procedures, may also apply.

Big Takeaways from Chapter 5

- Your preferences may guide a design, but they should not overshadow the patterns revealed in the preferences of those who will actually engage with a design. Since design should be iterative, decisions made along the way need to be made with careful and ethical interpretation of data.
- For big decisions that impact the design the most, systematic data wherein the researchers can feel confident that they've captured a clear and present pattern in attitudes or experiences is ideal.
- As the design process unfolds, at each step designers ought to present findings from the previous step as explicit justification for design decisions. This is socially-informed research not just because the people who will be engaging with a design have had their voices included in the design process, but because the designers explicitly talk about the inclusion of these findings as they propose their design. This is a case not just of doing the research, but talking about the research outcomes with those who participated in it.

Why Does All of This Matter, Again? Socially-Informed Research in Design

Sometimes designs don't work for everyone, even if all the steps of socially-informed research in the design process are followed. Recently, a student of mine told me that a new residence hall on campus did not do a good job of fostering community and inclusion. He wrote to me because he knew of my interest in this kind of topic, but he didn't know that I had been part of the design process in the first place – a design process where fostering community and inclusion was a central goal! I told him I'd love to talk about this with him sometime, since (a) these topics matter a lot to me and (b) sometimes we don't always get things right for everyone who eventually resides in the buildings that are designed. Of course, because I am not aware of any formal post-occupancy study of the building's efficacy that was shared with those of us who participated in the research that informed the design, I have no way of knowing whether his sentiments are representative of other students. Even if this student's ideas are not representative of most students' views, I very much look forward to this conversation so that I can figure out what the issues may be, and so that I can use what I learn to inform any future work I do with designers (and maybe even help sort out improvements in the current building). I tell this story to remind you that we are all human, and that it is impossible to meet everyone's needs all of the time. But if we at least infuse socially-informed research into design as much as possible, we are more likely to meet more people's needs, and thus more likely to make designs more socially sustainable (even with an occasional critic).

Sociology is not the only disciplinary lens that can be integrated with existing knowledge in architecture and interior design. As I have delved more deeply into the intersections of sociological research with user experience (UX) and human-centered design, I have found resources that interrogate how data itself is a social phenomenon to be the most useful. In particular, D'Ignazio and Klein (2020) organize much of what I offer in this book in a helpful set of principles that guide what they call "data feminism." I paraphrase these principles here:

1. Examine power (recognize that it matters in our world)
2. Challenge power (work toward justice by challenging inequality)
3. Elevate emotion and embodiment (value multiple forms of knowledge)
4. Rethink binaries and hierarchies (challenge systems of counting that may exacerbate inequalities)
5. Embrace pluralism (multiple perspectives are always better, especially if they come from localized ways of knowing)
6. Consider context (data are not neutral, but rather are products of social relationships that are unequal)
7. Make labor visible (the work of data science should be recognized and valued) (17–18)

I appreciate this list because it maps well onto the approach I take in socially-informed research throughout this book, especially considering inequalities, transparency, collaboration, inclusivity, and context. As I said in the Introduction, not all data is useful (and not all data should be collected). Making sure data is meaningful, accessible, measurable, and trackable over time – all while recognizing the process of data collection and analysis that may inform design is itself situated in our social world – is of utmost importance for researchers. Involving multiple voices in the design process, including that of the designers themselves and anyone whose voice may be unlikely to be included or heard, is key.

Designs should be flexible enough that anyone who engages with them can find use and enjoyment, regardless of experience, background, or ability. I have paired sociological methodological techniques, steps, and ideas in this book with stories from people in varied professional fields, including architecture, interior design, market research, health care, higher education, hospitality, museum curatorial work, the home building industry, community organization, and human-centered and UX design. My goal with this book has been to describe the inherent value designers bring to the table, and articulate how effective sociologically-informed data collection, analysis, and presentation can highlight this value to current and future clients and occupants. In this sense, I address the interplay between social and design values in professions dedicated to enhanced quality of life in our communities.

References

Bollo, Christina. 2021. "The Measure of Success." Paper presented at the American Institute of Architects National Housing Awards (online). May 3. https://network.aia.org/viewdocument/aia-national-housing-awards?CommunityKey=3934f0d4-c0c1-4600-b8a2-844131ba8365&tab=librarydocuments.

D'Ignazio, Catherine, and Lauren F. Klein. 2020. *Data Feminism*. Cambridge: The MIT Press.

Glossary

Affinity maps   a research method whereby participants put their ideas on post-it notes, and these are shared and organized or clustered into common themes.

Anonymity   when researchers do not know the identity of any participant, which is possible with survey methods where IP addresses and other identifying information are excluded from data collection. This is different from confidentiality, which protects the identity of participants but where the researcher knows who they are.

Applied sociologist   a sociologist dedicated to solving community problems and issues by using sociological theories and methods to do so, often to meet immediate needs of a client rather than to answer a research question for a peer-reviewed academic publication or presentation.

Architectural research (from Lucas)   studying the history and bodies of knowledge within the field of architecture, understanding the social and cultural context and the role of buildings in these contexts, and testing and improving theories about the meaning of the built environment for those who dwell in it.

Attributes   the "scores" along a variable (such as green or blue or purple for favorite color).

Bias   subjective opinions that may sway the outcomes of research.

Bivariate analysis   analysis of two variables together.

Card sorting activities   a UX or HCD research method where participants are given cards that are either blank with a call for them to note salient words or observations from a given set of ideas or that include salient choices on them that they then sort, prioritize, or cluster with others.

Closed-ended question questions on research instruments where all answer choices are provided for the research participant.

Code co-occurrence in qualitative research, the raw data (often in the form of text excerpts) that is coded into multiple codes at the same time.

Coding the process of turning the data as it comes to the researcher in raw form into data that is more manageable to organize, cluster, analyze numerically, and present in terms of patterns.

Coding round a step where the researcher carefully codes all of the text or other content being analyzed, noting patterns, and building off of previous rounds.

Confidentiality when researchers know who the participants in the research are (as when we do face-to-face interviews) but do not disclose their identities to others outside of the project.

Content analysis systematic analysis and coding of "texts" that people produce – writings, images, documents, artifacts, drawings – to find patterns.

Convenience sampling a sampling technique wherein researchers include participants who are convenient to reach, either because they are available and interested, or they are the ones who researchers are able to contact.

Cross-sectional research research that is done in one moment in time (or within a short period) that captures a snapshot of participants' attitudes, behaviors, and/or experiences at that moment.

Cultural capital (from Bourdieu) the social, material, and even linguistic resources someone has that make others see them as having higher status, which in turn brings them even more resources.

Cultural contexts shared value, belief, and language systems that provide the context for research and design processes.

Culture how a group makes meaning and demonstrates larger values of a society, including values, beliefs, customs, language, and the established way of doing things in everyday life.

Data input gathered in a systematic way from people participating in research.

Data cleaning the process wherein a dataset (usually quantitative, but can be qualitative) is put into a form where participants are de-identified (removing names, IP addresses, specific job titles, or other identifying information to keep people's responses confidential), where unnecessary metadata is removed (such as the timestamp of a survey), and where any variables that are included in text form (e.g., "yes" or "no") are recoded into numbers (yes = 1, no = 2) for any quantitative analyses that require statistical procedures beyond simply counting the number of each type of response.

Data visualization (sometimes called "data viz") graphic and visual representation of data to make a data story accessible to a wide audience, even among those who do not have an understanding of statistical procedures.

Deductive research when researchers start with hypotheses or theories that dictate what codes and patterns should be used and tested within the data and then move to data collection and analysis.

Defamiliarization (from Bauman and May) a process in sociological analysis which allows researchers to understand the underlying structures of the social world by puzzling over taken-for-granted, subtle, and even invisible aspects. These aspects – cultural rules for how we live together, social roles prescribed by our group identities, and social location based on finances, gender, or other demographic traits – are what sociologists notice when they tell the story of how a design is or is not working.

Descriptive research data collection and analysis that uncovers details related to what, who, where, when, and sometimes how things occur.

Descriptive/analytic method of qualitative data coding (from Gibbs) a method of thematic coding and categorizing of qualitative data that requires researchers to think about how data can be examined as surface-level descriptions and under-the-surface themes with meaning that can only be discovered by coding through several rounds.

Double-barreled question a question on a research instrument where respondents are asked about more than one variable in the same question, which prevents the capacity of a researcher to glean what people's answers mean in any sensible way.

Emic research a research approach that requires the researcher to be embedded within the group, activity, or culture being studied.

Empathy the ability to see yourself in someone else's shoes and to understand what others are experiencing.

Empathy maps visualization tools that help researchers summarize and make sense of what users convey during design research, and which offer a way to articulate this to various audiences in order to meet users' needs.

Empirical data that can be verified through observation or experience using any of the five senses.

Epistemology a theory of knowledge that incorporates the position that how we come to know what we know shapes how we approach our projects.

Ethnographic research a research method that includes deep, frequent, and systematic observation of people's behaviors and experiences at a site of interest.

Etic research a research approach where the researcher remains outside the group, activity, or culture being examined.

Exhaustive when a closed-ended question on a research instrument includes a complete list of answer choices, such that anyone who answers the question can find a response choice that matches their answer.

Exhibits a method common in architecture and design fields which consists of showcasing a design in some kind of visual format (drawings, animations, slides, 3-D renderings, full-size mock-ups), and then asking people to respond to the design.

Expertise the set of a designer's credentials, approaches, and knowledge that inform their design.

Explanatory Research data collection and analysis that uncovers details related to why things occur, such that explanation and prediction for future occurrences are both possible.

Feed-forward design (from Bollo) an approach to design wherein the designer incorporates or "feeds" ideas learned in the design process from one project into future designs.

Focus group interviews a research method that involves question-and-answer conversations between interviewers and a group of interviewees aimed at systematically eliciting and noticing patterns across interviewee responses and noting group-specific needs of those people who are interviewed.

Gallery walks organized meanderings of a group who is asked to respond to some kind of displayed content, often done in round robin or station-to-station fashion.

Human-centered design (HCD) designing an artifact (a building, a website, and even a new social system) by studying what users want, need, and do in order to inform the design in iterative steps throughout the design process.

Inductive research when researchers start with data collection and then analyze the data in order to lead to an explanation for what is happening (and why).

Informed consent as part of ethical research best practices, this entails researchers offering potential participants a verbal or written narrative explaining the risks and benefits of participating in the research, researcher contact information or support resources in case the research is troubling or traumatic, and the opportunity for the participant to skip any part of the research or opt out entirely.

Interval-ratio variable a variable where the attributes (or possible answers) are numbers and with which a mathematical mean can be calculated.

Interviews a research method that involves question-and-answer conversations between interviewers and interviewees aimed at systematically eliciting and noticing patterns across interviewee responses that go beyond noting individual needs of those people who are interviewed.

Interview guide   the list of questions researchers ask in an interview, sometimes referred to as an interview protocol or schedule.

Judgment sampling   a sampling technique wherein researcher or stakeholder expertise and social connections are used to decide what types of people to include in the research.

Level of measurement   a way to classify variables by type – in this case, whether the variable is a category, a ranking, or a number where a mathematical mean can be calculated.

Literature review   a brief summary of past research organized into themes, all of which justify the importance of a research question, offer background information to understand all of the factors that go into the question and point to places where the research may be missing new or better data.

Longitudinal research   research where data is collected or tracked over time.

Matrix or composite question   grouping a set of questions on a research instrument together such that, when added together, they make up a bunch of small factors that tell the story of a larger factor. This is sometimes referred to as a scale variable.

Measures of central tendency   the average, middle value, or most common response that show how an overall sample looks "on average" or "for the most part"), which can provide a quick story about overall patterns in the data. Measures of central tendency include means, medians, and modes.

Multistage sampling   sampling technique that involves including different types of sampling, each occurring at different stages in the design process.

Mutually exclusive   when a closed-ended question on a research instrument includes answers that do not overlap in any mathematical or conceptual way.

Nominal or categorical variables   variables that are measured as categories, where the answer choices (or attributes) are not ranked.

Non-probability samples   a sample wherein people are not given an equal chance to be included in the research.

Open-ended questions   questions in a research instrument that ask respondents for answers that they provide in narrative form (written or oral).

Open/axial/selective coding method   (from Williams and Moser) a method of qualitative data analysis that requires multiple rounds of coding to understand patterns and meaning in the data that move from description of common words or phrases to deeper themes that connect codes.

Operationalization the process of changing an abstract concept into a measurable variable.

Ordinal variable a variable where the attributes are ranked, but not necessarily numeric.

Personas a technique wherein fictional characters or created profiles that are composites of real data from people who may engage with your design in certain ways are used to make design decisions.

Positionality the ways that the social position of a researcher relates to the people involved in the research (or the community context in which the research is taking place).

Post-occupancy data data that is collected after people have moved into a building or engaged with a design once completed.

Post-occupancy evaluation research conducted after a design is completed to see if the goals of the design have been met.

Probability sampling sampling wherein everyone has an equal probability (or chance) of being selected.

Prompts within a set of interview questions, notes to the researcher to be sure and follow up with certain questions depending on interviewees' answers.

Qualitative data data that is akin to a set of stories or subjective experiences; patterns may be noted but more likely the main goal is depth and context rather than counting frequencies.

Quantitative data data that is made up of numbers, sometimes paired with sophisticated statistical analyses after data is collected.

Quota sample a sampling technique wherein researchers make sure that at least someone from each of any relevant stakeholder groups is included in the research, but the people chosen within the subgroups are chosen not by chance but by some other factors (e.g., availability, preference for inclusion by supervisors, interest in the project).

Random sampling a sampling technique which allows for statistical generalizability because everyone in a population has an equal chance of being included in the research.

Reflexivity when a researcher is aware of the role that their presence in the research process may shape how participants respond, and then adjusts the research approach to lessen bias.

Reliability when a researcher operationalizes variables and gets consistent answers each time the variable is used across studies.

Representativeness when the people in the sample closely match the traits of the population of interest.
Research a scientific approach in the design process that includes posing good questions, collecting and analyzing appropriate data, and interpreting and sharing findings using concepts and theories that come from fields that relate to the question.
Research ethics the formal and informal rules used to ensure that research is conducted legally, compassionately, and justly.
Sample a subset of a population included in a research project in order to make claims about a larger population that the sample is supposed to represent.
Skip pattern *or* contingency question a question or set of questions in a research instrument wherein people are shown certain questions depending on how they answer an earlier question.
Snowball sampling a sampling technique wherein people who participate in the research are asked to "spread the word" about the research and help identify (and sometimes contact) others who may be eligible and interested in participating.
Social inequalities when groups of people have unequal access to valuable resources such as money, space, or time.
Social structures ways that society is organized.
Socially-informed research in design the ethical and intentional incorporation of human-centered data gathering and analysis throughout the design process. It is the iterative and systematic practice of gathering, analyzing, and sharing input from people who occupy and engage with the built environments that architects and interior designers create as the designs are created and built.
Sociological imagination (from Mills) a skill that allows us to understand any experience by considering both personal stories and the larger social and historical contexts in which those stories take place.
Sociology the scientific study of human group behavior.
Straight-lining in survey research, when people check the same column over and over without looking at what they are answering, thus not giving accurate responses.
Stratified random sampling a sampling technique wherein researchers pick a random sample within each of the subsets (or "strata") that they want to be represented in the research.
Systematic sampling a sampling technique that is similar to random sampling and is considered to be a type of probability sampling using lists of potential participants but may lack representativeness because of how a list of people may be organized.

Time-use studies or diaries data gathering tools wherein the research participant makes notes or responds to quick questions throughout the time period under investigation.

Triangulation using more than one research method to answer a question

Unit of analysis the size of the entity – individual or group – that, when collected or aggregated, makes up a sample being studied.

Univariate analysis data analysis of one variable.

Universal design design that is flexible enough that anyone who engages with the design can find it easy to use and enjoyable, regardless of ability.

Validity when a researcher operationalizes a variable such that it is the closest possible proxy for the actual meaning of that variable; in other words, when a variable actually measures what it is supposed to measure.

Variable a characteristic that varies from unit of analysis to unit of analysis; a feature or factor that changes "scores" from person to person or group to group.

Index

Note: **Bold** page numbers refer to tables

access 21, 40, 42, 104
aesthetics 73–74
affinity maps 67
American Institute of Architects research 10
American Sociological Association Code of Ethics 68
analytic coding 126–127
anecdotal evidence 90
anonymity 50
applied sociologist 23
Architectural research 7–8
architecture 2, 4, 5, 7–11, 15–18, 24, 26–28, 35, 36, 42, 53, 79–80, 112, 116, 136, 144, 155

Bettison-Varga, Lori 11, 106
bias 77–78
bivariate analysis 60, 69
Blessing, Shelby 2
body of knowledge 8
Body-Lawson, Victor 142
Bollo, Christina 45–46, 114
Bourdieu, Pierre 21
Bradbury, Simon 17
builder-client relationship 26

card sorting activities 69
categorical/nominal variable 123
central limit theorem 41
Chou, Jou-Yie 143

Christopherson, Neal 129
closed-ended questions 56–57, 63–65
coding 122–130
communication 90–93, 149
confidentiality 50, 105
constant comparison method 128
content analysis, texts, maps, drawing/documents 70–71; benefits and drawbacks **55**; timing and pace, data collection 110–111
Contract Design Network 10
convenience sampling 86
COVID-19 23–24, 53, 56, 97, 100–101, 114, 143
critical thinking 22
cross-sectional research 107
cultural capital 21, 24, 94
cultural context 19, 98

D'Ignazio, Catherine 155
Dam, Rikke Friis 22
Danish National Gallery of Art (Statens Museum for Kunst) 1
data analysis 16, 27, 37, 40, 47, 55, 60, 74–75, 115, 116, 118, 131, 136, 137; data presentation 154; digital 133–135; probability/non-probability sample 149; qualitative 124–126, 128; quantitative 122–124
data cleaning 122

Index

data collection (or data gathering) 22, 53–55, 97, 120, 122, 123, 131, 136, 145, 147–148, 151; access 73–74, 104; and analysis 7, 23, 30, 37, 80, 155, 156; design and methods 3; designing 147–148; ethical and empathetic 82; timing and pace 106–116; tools 74; and triangulation 71–73; using content analysis 70–71; using focus groups 66–68; using interviews 61–66; using observation 68–70; using surveys 56–62
data feminism 155
data files and storage systems 48–49
data story 152–154
data visualization 115, 118, 119, 134, 135, 137–140
data-driven culture 4, 5, 32
data-informed design 27
Dedoose 135
deductive analysis 127
defamiliarization 21
democratic design 141
descriptive coding 126–127
design equity 142
design thinking 22
designer role 77–82; and expertise 34–36; and inequality and power 93–95
designer-client-user relationships 16
digital data analysis 133–135
display logic 60
double-barreled questions 59

emic research 80–82
empathy 81–82; maps 128–130
empirical data 31
epistemology 31
ethnography 68, 102–103; timing and pace, data collection 110
etic research 80–82
evidence-based design 4, 9, 18
exhibits 69

feed-forward design 45, 46, 115, 135–136
focus group interviews 66–68; benefits and drawbacks 55
for-profit/not-for-profit work 25

gallery walks 69–70
geographic context 98
Gibbs, Graham R. 126, 132
global health crisis 101

hard sciences 4
Hatleskog, Eli 10
Hay, Rowena 17
Hospitality Diversity Action Council 143
human-centered design (HCD) 3, 9, 11, 16, 22–23, 28, 49, 55, 67, 81, 93, 94, 108, 121, 148, 155
Hunter-Cuyjet, Sequoyah 142

inclusivity 15–16, 143
individual interviews 61–66; benefits and drawbacks 55; timing and pace, data collection 109–110
inductive analysis 127
informed consent 95
input-gathering process 94
Institutional Review Board 50, 136
interior design 4–7, 9–11, 17, 18, 24–27, 113, 155, 156
interval-ratio variable 41

Janning, Marty 93
judgment sampling 86

Khanani, Fauzia 6
Klein, Lauren F. 155
knowledge tradition 8

Lawrence, Damon 92, 144
level of measurement 40–41
literature review 46
location-based methods 101–104
longitudinal research 107
Lucas, Ray 7–9, 42

mapping social values 10
matrix/composite question 58
Mills, C. Wright 21
multistage sampling 86

Natural History Museum (NHM) 11
Nickerson, Romano 54, 72–73, 93, 121
Nielsen, Jakob 17, 88
non-probability samples 85, 86, 149
NVivo 135

observation 68–70; benefits and drawbacks 55; timing and pace, data collection 110
on-site *vs.* off-site 101–104
Open Architecture Collaborative 10
open/axial/selective coding 127–128

open-concept work space 47
open-ended questions 57, 63–65, 69
operationalization 38
ordinal variable 40, 124

pandemic 23–24
panel study 107
participatory design 5
Pathways to Equity program 10
pen-and-paper analysis 132–133
personas 121
population 57
positionality 78
post-occupancy data 2, 155
post-occupancy evaluation (POE) 106–107, 113
probability sampling 84–85, 149
probability theory 41
project management platform 49
projects, motivations and goals 14, **14**
public/private boundaries 101–104, 105–106

qualitative data analysis 7, 54, 74, 124–126, 128, 130–131, 136
Quality of Life Foundation 10
Qualtrics 60, 134
quantitative data analysis 7, 54, 74, 122–124, 130–131, 136
quota sample 85

Rachie, Jaimie Thimmesh 76
random sampling 84
recoding 123
reflexivity 79
reliability 57
representativeness 57, 84
research ethics 49–50, 77–79, 82, 119–121
research question 7, 43, 47, 52, 53, 75, 82, 108, 121, 145, 146, 152–153
Rodhouse, Joseph 58

sample 57, 82–90, 149; size 87–90; *see also individual types*
Samuel, Flora 10, 17
scale variable 58
selective coding 128
semi-standardized interviews 64
Siang, Teo Yu 22
Silverstein 113
skip logic 60
skip pattern/contingency question 60

snowball sampling 86
social inequalities 6, 9, 15, 18–20, 32, 82, 142, 144
social media feeds 56
social research methods 6, 16–18, 31, 50, 51
social scientific methods 13, 17, 28
social structures 19
socially-informed research 12, 95, 144, 148; for architects and interior designers 27, 28, 143; data analysis 115, 151; data collection 71–72, 152; in design 5, 18, 25, 26, 31, 32, 37–41, 51, 54, 57, 58, 70, 77–78, 81, 82, 98, 99, 103, 104, 106, 114, 116, 120, 136, 137, 154–156
sociological imagination 21, 22
sociologist 13, 23, 24, 31–32, 141
sociology 2, 6, 8, 9–11, 13, 16, 17, 46, 128, 155; applied sociology 22–23; design 18–22, 24; professional ethics 102; thesis projects 30, 44
socio-political context 12
stakeholder 35–36
stakeholder mapping 83–84
statistical significance tests 41
Stevenson, Fionn 10
stratified random sampling 85
surveys 56–61; benefits and drawbacks **55**; timing and pace, data collection 109
sustainability 15, 18, 28, 94, 143
systematic research 7
systematic sampling 85

Tableau 137
Tar Pits project 11
Thomas, Crystal Vinisse 144
time-use studies/diaries 111
timing and pace, data collection 106–109, 150–152; after the design 113–114; content analysis 110–111; before the design 112; during the design 113; ethnography 110; interviews 109–110; observation 110; pre- and post-tests alignment 114; surveys 109
transparency 50–51, 78, 93, 95
triangulation 71–73
trust 104–105

UK Collaborative Centre for Housing Evidence 10
unit of analysis 37–38
univariate analysis 60, 69

universal design 33
UX (user experience design) 3, 22, 67, 83–84, 108; and empathy maps 128–129; and sample size 88–89

validity 57
variable 38

Van der Ryn 113
Vetter, McKenna 79–80, 121

Watson, Kelly J. 17
Wearing, Gillian 1, 2
work/personal/family time 100

For Product Safety Concerns and Information please contact our EU representative GPSR@taylorandfrancis.com
Taylor & Francis Verlag GmbH, Kaufingerstraße 24, 80331 München, Germany

www.ingramcontent.com/pod-product-compliance
Lightning Source LLC
Chambersburg PA
CBHW070616300426
44113CB00010B/1549